POST COMPULSORY
TEACHER EDUCATORS

Connecting professionals

Critical Guides for
Teacher Educators

You might also like the following books from Critical Publishing

Ability Grouping in Primary Schools: Case Studies and Critical Debates
Rachel Marks
978-1-910391-24-2

Beginning Teachers' Learning: Making Experience Count
Katharine Burn, Hazel Hagger and Trevor Mutton
978-1-910391-17-4

Coteaching in Teacher Education: Innovative Pedagogy for Excellence
Colette Murphy
978-1-910391-82-2

Developing Creative and Critical Educational Practitioners
Victoria Door
978-1-909682-37-5

Developing Outstanding Practice in School-based Teacher Education
Edited by Kim Jones and Elizabeth White
978-1-909682-41-2

How Do Expert Primary Classteachers Really Work? A Critical Guide for Teachers, Headteachers and Teacher Educators
Tony Eaude
978-1-909330-01-6

Teacher Status and Professional Learning: The Place Model
Linda Clarke
978-1-910391-46-4

Theories of Professional Learning
Carey Philpott
978-1-909682-33-7

Our titles are also available in a range of electronic formats. To order please go to our website www.criticalpublishing.com or contact our distributor NBN International by telephoning 01752 202301 or emailing orders@nbninternational.com.

POST COMPULSORY
TEACHER EDUCATORS

Connecting professionals

Series Editor: Ian Menter

Critical Guides for
Teacher Educators

Jim Crawley

First published in 2016 by Critical Publishing Ltd

British Library Cataloguing in Publication Data
A CIP record for this book is available from the British Library

ISBN: 978-1-910391-86-0

This book is also available in the following e-book formats:
MOBI: 978-1-910391-87-7
EPUB: 978-1-910391-88-4
Adobe e-book reader: 978-1-910391-89-1

Cover and text design by Greensplash Limited
Project Management by Out of House Publishing
Typeset by Newgen Knowledge Works Pvt. Ltd.
Print Managed and Manufactured by Jellyfish Solutions

Critical Publishing
3 Connaught Road
St Albans
AL3 5RX

www.criticalpublishing.com

CONTENTS

FOREWORD

Since launching the series *Critical Guides for Teacher Education* in 2014, the need for such volumes seems to have increased yet more. When we started the series we were acutely aware that there were many parts of the world where teacher education was becoming increasingly diverse in its organisation, structure and curriculum. Furthermore, an increasing range of participants were being asked to take responsibility for supporting the introduction of new members into the profession and for ensuring their continuing learning and development. It is certainly my belief that earlier volumes in the series have helped enormously in providing the kinds of research-based insights that will support the development of high-quality teacher learning and development in whatever context it is taking place.

The books have always been cognisant of the benefits of international research and experience in teacher education and are being well received in many parts of the world. Their emphasis on criticality is also very important in today's world where politicians often promulgate simple, indeed simplistic, answers to the 'policy problem' of teacher education.

We can see how important such work is when we read global overviews of teacher education policy and practice such as that provided by Darling-Hammond and Lieberman (2012). But we can also see how rich the context of the United Kingdom and the Republic of Ireland is, when analysing what is happening in the five nations: England, Northern Ireland, Scotland, Wales and the Republic of Ireland, as demonstrated in the recent work *Teacher Education in Times of Change* (Teacher Education Group, 2016).

Similarly, the widely cited report of the inquiry undertaken by the British Educational Research Association (BERA) in collaboration with the Royal Society for the Arts, Manufacture and Commerce (RSA) (BERA-RSA, 2014) has offered evidence for the importance of a systematic approach to the use of research and evidence in high-quality teacher education.

It is therefore a great pleasure to introduce the first volume in the series to focus very directly on a much neglected sector of teacher education, that of post compulsory education (PCE). As Jim Crawley and his colleagues argue throughout the book, the PCE sector of teacher education has been very much the 'poor relation' or 'Cinderella' of teacher education. Furthermore, if teacher education for schools has been the object of maverick meddling by politicians for many years now, most especially in England, PCE has been at least as much the subject of a relentless stream of policy interventions – and not only in England. This is a huge sector of education which, from being much neglected over many decades has become a focus of interest for many politicians and has been the site for the creation of one new agency after another.

The volume therefore provides an enormously valuable resource in offering a clear, thoughtful and deeply committed analysis of teacher education in this sector and of the professional identities and responsibilities of those who work in it.

Ian Menter, Series Editor
Emeritus Professor of Teacher Education, University of Oxford

REFERENCES

BERA-RSA (2014) *Research and the Teaching Profession – Building Capacity for a Self-improving Education System*. London: BERA (available at www.bera.ac.uk/wp-content/uploads/2013/12/BERA-RSA-Research-Teaching-Profession-FULL-REPORT-for-web.pdf (accessed September 2016)).

Darling-Hammond, L and Lieberman, A (eds) (2012) *Teacher Education around the World*. London: Routledge.

The Teacher Education Group (2016) *Teacher Education in Times of Change*. Bristol: Policy Press.

About the series editor

Ian Menter is Emeritus Professor of Teacher Education and was formerly the Director of Professional Programmes in the Department of Education at the University of Oxford. He previously worked at the Universities of Glasgow, the West of Scotland, London Metropolitan, the West of England and Gloucestershire. Before that he was a primary school teacher in Bristol, England. His most recent publications include *A Literature Review on Teacher Education for the 21st Century* (Scottish Government) and *A Guide to Practitioner Research in Education* (Sage). His work has also been published in many academic journals.

About the book editor

Jim Crawley is a senior lecturer in education studies and teaching fellow at Bath Spa University. He has over 35 years of teaching experience, including teacher education, basic skills and adult and community learning. He co-ordinated post compulsory teacher education at Bath Spa University for 12 years, gaining two Ofsted outstanding grades during that time. Jim was chair of the Post-16 Committee of the Universities' Council for the Education of Teachers (UCET) between 2012 and 2015. He is the founder member and now convener of a national research network (Teacher Education in Lifelong Learning – TELL) with over 200 members and convener of the South West Regional Teacher Educators' Forum. Jim gained his PhD with a thesis on *The professional situation of teacher educators in the lifelong learning sector* in November 2014 and is a very active researcher in the field.

ABOUT THE **CONTRIBUTORS**

Carol Azumah Dennis began working for the University of Hull as a programme director for post-16 education and training in 2010. This followed several years of working in further, adult and community education as a teacher and manager. Her doctorate explored the ways in which the rage for accountability impacted upon the professional lives and identities of those working in further education (FE). She now teaches, researches and writes about post-16 education and takes every opportunity to ensure the sector engages with and responds to policy.

Vicky Duckworth is a senior lecturer and research fellow at Edge Hill University, UK. Throughout her career Vicky has published widely for the post compulsory sector, including texts on adult basic skills and adult literacy. She is deeply committed to challenging inequality through critical and emancipatory approaches to education, widening participation, inclusion, community action and engaging in research with a strong social justice agenda.

Rebecca Eliahoo is a principal lecturer (lifelong learning) at the University of Westminster in London and has led a post compulsory teacher education consortium since 2008. She researches mentors' experiences supporting trainees during initial teacher training, and completed a thesis on the professional development needs of teacher educators for her PhD. In 2003 she won a Walter Hines Page scholarship to study language and widening participation in the recruitment of teachers in Texas, USA, and in both 2005 and 2011 she was awarded a teaching fellowship for excellence in teaching and learning.

Lynn Machin is an award leader, senior lecturer and a PhD, EdD, MA supervisor at Staffordshire University. She has more than 25 years' experience of working within further and higher education. Many of these years have been spent designing and delivering initial teacher training for trainees who work, or want to work, in the FE sector. Her post-doctoral research interests are situated in the exploration of how students can develop their capacities to learn and grow as self-directed and autonomous learners.

Kevin Orr is a reader in work and learning at the University of Huddersfield. Prior to joining the university he taught in FE colleges around Manchester for 16 years, mainly on ESOL and teacher education provision. He still maintains a keen interest in FE and recently co-edited the book, *Further Education and the Twelve Dancing Princesses*, which provides a defence of the sector and a vision of how it might be. In 2014 he was awarded a National Teaching Fellowship by the Higher Education Academy (HEA).

Denise Robinson entered FE teaching in 1975 and moved into teacher education and professional development in 1987. She was employed as a regional adviser on teacher education reforms to both FENTO and LLUK and until very recently was the director of a large teacher education partnership. She was awarded a National Teaching Fellowship by the HEA for her work in widening participation. Denise continues to contribute and work in the sector through her writing on teacher education, and as an external examiner and speaker.

Nena Skrbic has been a teacher educator in the education and training sector for ten years. Her doctorate is in English language and literature and she has delivered both subject-specialist and generic programmes of initial teacher preparation (ITP) since 2005. One of Nena's research interests is how learning to teach is understood by teacher educators and their trainees. She is curriculum area manager for teacher education at Leeds City College.

CHAPTER 1 | INTRODUCING THE 'INVISIBLE EDUCATORS'

Jim Crawley

CRITICAL **ISSUES**

- *What is unique about post compulsory education (PCE) teacher education and about PCE teacher educators (TEds)?*

- *What makes PCE TEds 'invisible educators'?*

- *What are the characteristics of PCE TEds?*

- *How can we enhance the value of PCE teacher education and PCE TEds?*

Introduction

The professional, educational and funding turbulence experienced by teacher education and teacher educators (TEds) across all sectors since 2008 has been significant. Austerity financing and increasing government intervention have provided many new and difficult challenges. At the same time, evidence is building that the quality of teaching is the most important contributor to the quality of learning and achievement (BERA-RSA, 2014). Teacher education is demonstrably one of the most important influences on that teaching quality. International research suggests that teacher education in the UK and internationally continues to support improvements in the quality of teachers and teaching despite operating in challenging times and circumstances (BERA-RSA, 2014).

At the same time, research suggests that TEds do not have a strong professional identity, and that they are 'semi-academics' who do not engage as often as other academics in research, and their activity as a coherent community of practice is limited (Boyd et al, 2011). A combination of these factors can render TEds to what could be described as 'invisible educators'. PCE TEds, even within the world of teacher education, often have the lowest visibility of all (Crawley, 2013, 2014; Noel, 2006).

This chapter introduces the key ideas and themes of this book and how the authors have combined to present a more visible, confident and outward-facing set of perspectives on the community of PCE TEds. The book is evidence of a shift in our psychology, approach and self-confidence, which although not at this stage seismic, is important and of significance to the cause of teacher education, and which forms a call to action for PCE.

What is unique about PCE teacher education and PCE TEds?

PCE teacher education and PCE TEds are both situated in a working environment which is particularly diverse, complex, dynamic and challenging. In Chapter 3, Orr charts and analyses this context when considering what the sector is for, who the sector is for and how the sector is changing. His account reinforces how difficult it is to answer these questions precisely, especially because of the bewildering frequency of change. In Chapter 4, Machin provides the historical context of the key policies affecting PCE teacher education from Butler in 1944 to Lingfield in 2012. Machin echoes Orr's conclusion that PCE has become 'pivotal' for governments in preparing people to gain the appropriate skills for the UK to compete in a global economy, and how government actions have not often been seen to help that aspiration.

In Chapters 2, 3, 4, 5 and 6, Dennis et al, Orr, Machin, Duckworth, and Robinson and Skrbic all include analysis of how PCE teacher education is inevitably affected by the sector context and close attention from governments. Being a part of a sector which is described as the 'filling in the educational sandwich' and the 'Cinderella' sector (Chapter 3, Orr) inevitably affects teacher education and these chapters explore those effects, and introduce some developments which have helped to mitigate their effects.

PCE teacher education

What is it?

This book uses an adapted version of Crawley's (2010) definition of post compulsory education to define PCE teacher education, which is:

If you are training teachers in further education, adult and community learning, workplace learning, 14–19 provision, public services training or offender learning which is not delivered by school teachers, you are working in post compulsory education teacher education.

At the time of writing, teacher education qualifications have been revised for the third time in 12 years, as outlined in Chapter 4 (Machin). They are at a range of levels, worth differing amounts of credit, and offer a step-by-step pathway to full qualification, usually to diploma at higher education (HE) level 5 or higher. Since 2012, gaining these qualifications is no longer a legal requirement for teachers, as is also described in Chapter 4. Qualifications are offered by universities and awarding organisations on a part-time and full-time basis. This combination of short and longer qualifications is unusual across global teacher education, but not thought to be entirely unique by Crawley (2013 and 2014).

Where does PCE teacher education happen, on what scale and in what conditions?

In Chapter 3, Orr makes it clear that good quality data about PCE is difficult to come by, but there have been some improvements in this area recently and it is possible from a number of sources to provide at least some data about PCE teacher education. It takes place in universities and in almost all other provider organisations across PCE including colleges, adult education services, private training providers, public sector organisations, prisons and armed forces establishments. Education and Training Foundation (2015) counted 829 providers in England in 2012/13. Crawley (2013) drew together data for each of the three consecutive years of 2008/9 to 2010/11. As many as 45,000 teachers in PCE were registered for teacher education qualifications in England for each of these three years. Almost 90 per cent of them were part-time in-service participants and over 55 per cent gained their qualifications through universities (LLUK, 2009, 2010, 2011). Although these numbers are difficult to compare with school teacher education, because of different funding, attendance and data gathering regimes (school teacher education has a 'comprehensive' governance regime and PCE does not), they clearly represent a significant amount of activity. Even with the impact of austerity measures and budget cuts, over 30,000 PCE teachers still gained teaching qualifications in 2012/13 (ETF, 2015).

In Chapters 2, 3, 5, 6 and 7, Dennis et al, Orr, Duckworth, Robinson and Skrbic, and Eliahoo, respectively, all highlight how the PCE sector conditions and mixed model of delivery are to some degree unique but that there are difficulties many TEds appear to encounter wherever they are working and whichever of the phases of teacher education they carry out. These include: a lack of research visibility and professional status; limited negotiating power and influence due to significant and growing government interference; and an ambivalence of position. It is possible for TEds to be seen as advocates for critical thinking, while at the same time part of the controls of managerialism afflicting the education sector. This uncertain terrain for teacher education is not unique to PCE, but is present in a more direct way when training teachers than when working as a teacher.

PCE TEds

If PCE is the Cinderella of English education more broadly, then PCE teacher education has always been the Cinderella of English teacher education. Time after time, PCE TEd practitioners attend conferences, events, consultations and other occasions where keynote national and international speakers, who are addressing *all of teacher education*, do not mention PCE teacher education, or the closely related vocational teacher education (even when they actually have very successful PCE provision within their own institution's portfolio). When ministers speak of teacher education, or governments report on teacher education, or teacher development in universities, PCE teacher education is rarely mentioned, partly due to the 'other people's children' problem but also due to the 'Cinderella' nature of the sector (both of these factors are further discussed in Chapter 3, Orr). The recent Carter Review of Initial Teacher Training (DfE, 2015), for example, mentions the word 'school' 366 times in its 81 pages. The word 'college' is mentioned, but not in any way associated with PCE. The report's foreword mentions how schools are '*at the heart of every community*' (DfE, 2015, p 1), but gives no mention to the colleges and other providers who also work hard to be part of that community.

It could be argued that PCE is different and requires different attention, but this is not an isolated incident. There have been specific reviews of policy and funding for PCE teacher education, but these have never been as wide-ranging as, or on a similar scale to, school-based teacher education. The funding of Centres for Excellence in Teacher Training (CETTs) in 2007 was generous in PCE terms at £30m over three years, but pales into insignificance when compared to the £300m over five years made available to universities to develop Centres for Excellence in Teaching and Learning (CETL).

In Chapter 2, Dennis et al demonstrate how this low sector profile is reinforced by a particularly low visibility in research activity and publication, or a '*scholarly silence*', and in Chapter 4, Machin outlines a history of change and reorganisation which has beset PCE TEds for more than 60 years. It is these factors which have conspired, along with the difficult professional and sector context, to make PCE TEds almost 'invisible' and in Chapters 2 and 6, Dennis et al and Robinson and Skrbic examine this invisibility in some depth.

When we review UK and international research, however, a series of positive shared themes, values and pedagogies do emerge for all of teacher education. In Chapter 2, Dennis et al discuss a quality which has been attributed to TEds called '*even more*' by Crawley (2013) and '*more than*' by Swennen (2014), which suggests the breadth and depth of their roles and responsibilities. In Chapter 5, Duckworth emphasises the significance of working towards improved social justice and empowering teachers through practitioner research and in Chapter 6, Robinson and Skrbic analyse modelling and the degree to which TEds can act as '*connecting professionals*' through their pedagogical principles and practices. In Chapter 7, Eliahoo uses international research evidence to explore the challenges and benefits of attempts to develop local, national and international collaboration between TEds and the ways in which this could enhance professional visibility and confidence for English TEds.

Overall the reflections on PCE teacher education and on the practices and principles of PCE TEds in this book reinforce the complexity, turbulent history and diverse challenges of their particular context and characterises their dispositions and values. A picture emerges of a group that has adopted a set of strategies, techniques and values to continue with their work, training a new generation of teachers, and contributing positively to the economic and human communities within which we live and work despite that difficult situation. This demonstrates their singular commitment to PCE, but also their recognisable connections and relevance to and for all of teacher education. In Chapter 8, Crawley explores this notion of TEds as connecting professionals further.

Enhancing the value of PCE teacher education and PCE TEds

PCE teacher education has moved forward significantly in the last ten years. The establishment of CETTs in 2009, although a flawed initiative as it was not truly national, and improving Ofsted grades for PCE TEds and their institutions (ETF, 2015; Ofsted, 2014) have raised the standard of initial teacher education (ITE) and contributed to improvements in teacher confidence and feelings of professionalism and the quality and consistency of continuing professional development. The short-lived requirement (from 2001 to 2012) for PCE teachers to become qualified, the mandatory declaration of continuing professional development (CPD) annually and a reasonable level of funding to support these developments all helped. Lingfield (BIS, 2012) dismissed these improvements, but their legacy still remains, and most PCE organisations are still training and qualifying their teachers (ETF, 2015). In Chapter 8 Crawley summarises some of these improvements and proposes next steps which could renew this improvement as the sector moves into an uncertain future.

TELLing our own story

As already indicated, TEds do not have a strong professional identity, and they are considered 'semi-academics' (Boyd et al, 2011) who do not engage as often as other academics in research. This book is evidence of how the community of PCE TEds has come together in order to enhance the research base of this field of endeavour, and this chapter closes with the story of the Teacher Education in Lifelong Learning (TELL) research network as one example of that effort.

In 2011, with a very small amount of funding, a conference was held in Wiltshire with the express purpose of seeking to establish a specialist research network for Lifelong Learning teacher education (what is called PCE teacher education in this book). No such network existed, and this was a call to the PCE TEd community to join together to take some of their own destiny in their hands. After a successful first meeting with over 50 participants, TELL was established with the objectives to:

» capture the passion and distinctive vision which permeates PCE teacher education;

» raise the profile of and celebrate PCE teacher education;

» build capacity, support and provide opportunities for practitioner researchers and research in the field of PCE teacher education;

» connect researchers across the UK with each other;

» promote the achievements and debate the challenges of PCE teacher education;

» make appropriate use of technology to connect and inform members, publish research information, updates and results; share issues, news and ideas and enable participation in the network, independent of geography;

» curate and collate PCE teacher education research, history and information including compiling a bank of ideas, publications and resources relating to teacher education and build a legacy of the work undertaken.

At the point of publication, the TELL network now has over 220 members across the country and across the sector. The growing body of research of and by the individual members, the joint ventures such as this book, the lively network meetings which are attended by some 150 people across each year and the improved connections between PCE TEds are all encouraging. Perhaps the most important reason for this is the completely voluntary nature of the network. It is self-managed and has no funding. It takes place because PCE TEds want it to, and it represents one of the few professional areas where we have some professional control over what we do.

IN A **NUTSHELL**

PCE teacher education operates in a difficult context, as does much other teacher education provision around the world. This situation is not necessarily likely to improve in the near future, and teacher education in England continues to experience more change and reorganisation than in many other countries.

Research on PCE teacher education, and particularly the TEds who work in it, is still relatively rare, and the professional situation of the TEds involved is not supportive for changing that situation. Despite this and because of the qualities and values you will find evidenced in this book, PCE TEds are enhancing their work and their research, and this book is one element of the proof of that.

REFLECTIONS ON **CRITICAL ISSUES**

There is a degree of uniqueness about PCE teacher education, and the situation of PCE TEds, but this appears to be more to do with the sector context rather than their characteristics, situation, disposition and values. There are however significant similarities between PCE TEds and other TEds, including their emphasis on the importance of social justice as a goal for education, use of modelling, their focus on supporting their students, and their 'evenmoreness'.

The factors which render PCE TEds as 'invisible educators' have been introduced, and these include low status, a low research profile and a lack of recognition even when good levels of improvement are made.

This book offers a practical, coherent, critical vision based on ideas and values around which practitioners can unite. Gleeson, Davies and Wheeler (2005, p 445) argue that difficult times can present opportunities for '*the making and taking of professionalism*', and the authors of this book believe that it is a pivotal moment for such a publication.

REFERENCES

BERA-RSA (British Educational Research Association – Royal Society of Arts) (2014) *Research and the Teaching Profession – Building the Capacity for a Self-improving Education System*. London: BERA / RSA.

BIS (Department of Business, Innovation and Skills) (2012) *Professionalism in Further Education – Final Report (Lingfield Report)*. London: BIS.

Boyd, P, Harris, K and Murray, J (2011) *Becoming a Teacher Educator: Guidelines for the Induction of Newly Appointed Lecturers in Initial Teacher Education* (2nd edn). Bristol: ESCalate.

Crawley, J (2010) *In at the Deep End: A Survival Guide for Teachers in Post Compulsory Education* (2nd edn). London: Routledge.

Crawley, J (2013) Endless Patience and a Strong Belief in What Makes a Good Teacher: Teacher Educators in Post-compulsory Education in England and Their Professional Situation. *Research in Post-Compulsory Education*, 18: 336–47.

Crawley, J (2014) *How can a deeper understanding of the professional situation of LLS teacher educators enhance their future support, professional development and working context?* PhD Thesis. Bath: Bath Spa University.

DfE (Department for Education) (2015) *Carter Review of Initial Teacher Training*. London: DfE.

ETF (Education and Training Foundation) (2015) *Initial Teacher Education Provision in FE and Skills: Baseline Report*. London: ETF.

Gleeson, D, Davies, J and Wheeler, E (2005). On the Making and Taking of Professionalism in the Further Education Workplace. *British Journal of Sociology of Education*, 26: 445–60.

LLUK (Lifelong Learning UK) (2009) *Further Education Workforce Data for England: An Analysis of the Staff Individualised Record Data 2007–2008*. Coventry: LLUK.

LLUK (Lifelong Learning UK) (2010) *Further Education Workforce Data for England: An Analysis of the Staff Individualised Record Data 2008–2009*. Coventry: LLUK.

LLUK (Lifelong Learning UK) (2011) *Further Education Workforce Data for England: An Analysis of the Staff Individualised Record Data 2009–2010*. Coventry: LLUK.

Noel, P (2006) The Secret Life of Teacher Educators: Becoming a Teacher Educator in the Learning and Skills Sector. *Journal of Vocational Education and Training*, 58: 151–70.

Ofsted (2014) *Teaching, Learning and Assessment in Further Education and Skills – What Works and Why*. London: Ofsted.

Swennen, A (2014) More than Just a Teacher: The Identity of Teacher Educators, in Jones, K and White, E (eds) *Developing Outstanding Practice in School-based Teacher Education*. Northwich: Critical Publishing.

Carol Azumah Dennis with Jane Ballans, Marie Bowie, Sally Humphries and Sandra Stones

CRITICAL ISSUES

- *What does the scholarly literature tell us about post compulsory teacher educators (TEds)?*

- *What research methods and methodologies enable the exploration of a scholarly silence?*

- *What is distinctive about post compulsory education (PCE) TEds' pedagogic being?*

The 'even more' quality

Critical question

➤ What are the essential characteristics of a good PCE TEd?

This chapter takes as its starting point a comment made during a series of workshops involving professional conversations with some 250 PCE TEds. The initial stages of Crawley's (2013) multi-method research project generated 15 'essential characteristics' of a good teacher educator. Amidst such items as *'innovative and charismatic'*, *'passionate about teaching'* and *'the ability to model good practice in teaching, and knowingly – praxis'* – appears an elusive *'even more'* quality.

The 'even more' quality (demonstrating a wide range of professional confidence as a good teacher, but 'even more' so).

(Crawley, 2013, p 341)

This 'even more' abstraction was later included as one survey item amid 15 other defining features of a good PCE TEd. Teacher educators were then invited to critically evaluate the degree to which they 'already had' or needed to 'develop further' qualities identified as an essential characteristic for the PCE TEd. It is worth noting that this is an experienced and confident group of successful teacher educators. Despite this, an elusive 'even more' quality – that something extra that teacher educators do or are – was identified by some 50 per cent of respondents as an area for further development. In this chapter I wish to explore the critical issue of elusive *'evenmoreness'.*

Critical question

➤ How can we grasp the elusive 'evenmoreness?'

It is worth noting that the willingness of a group of experienced and accomplished professionals to count themselves as deficient in a quality that has no clear definition might be reflective of the extent to which PCE TEds have internalised the *'discourse of derision'* (Ball, 1990: 18) that has eroded the professional standing of teachers (and therefore teacher educators) across all phases of education over the past three decades. Morley and Rasool (2000) suggest this willingness to accept a self as in deficit and in perpetual need of improvement (without being able to precisely define improvement) as a powerful regulatory device. Attention paid to a self in perpetual need of improvement is attention shifted away from values and ideologies. This notion of the professional self as a diminished self in deficit might reasonably be compared to the Christian doctrine of original sin. It induces a passive resignation that focusses on technical and operational effectiveness rather than subversion and the creation of critical public spaces for dissent (Dennis, 2015).

As I attempt to pin down the elusive 'evenmoreness', I suggest the ambiguity reflects a broader – more focussed scholarly silence surrounding the PCE TEd. This scholarly silence resonates throughout the teacher education literature. To illustrate: in 2010 in response to an identified lacuna in scholarship around *'the role, development and professional identity of teacher educators'* (Swennen and Bates, 2010, p 1), the journal *Professional Development in Education* published a special edition which aimed to explore the professional development needs of teacher educators. Given my interest in the elusive 'evenmoreness' these 21 carefully curated papers might have been a good starting place to find out what additional development was required when PCE teachers became PCE TEds. What is stark about this special edition is that it does not feature a single contribution on vocational, further or adult education or any of its international institutional counterparts. The normative definition of a teacher educator is someone who prepares young adults to teach in primary or secondary school. Faced with such a scholarly silence it is no wonder that the PCE TEd may experience a crisis in confidence.

This chapter and the volume within which it appears emerge from this scholarly silence to elaborate upon the 'evenmoreness' of the PCE TEd's being.

The voice of PCE TEds

What research methods enable the application of the voice of PCE TEds?

Before elaborating upon the evenmoreness of the PCE TEds' being, it is important to address the question of how. That is, how might I grasp the evenmoreness to amplify these voices? What research methodologies enable a trustworthy and plausible exploration of the PCE TEds' being? The 'reflective practitioner' disposition has since the 1980s (Korthagen, 1995) achieved an iconic status in the literature surrounding PCE. This capacity to critically self-reflect is partly what defines the PCE teachers and teacher educators' being. It is unsurprising therefore that in the special edition noted above – self-study is by far the most popular research method. I am suggesting here that a quality strongly associated with being a TEd, 'critical reflection', also forms a strong basis for an approach to research and scholarship in teacher education: self-study.

Raising the voice of the PCE TEd

My methodology aligns itself broadly to collective auto-ethnography: interviews, self-interviews and group discussions. My data have been generated through a series of conversations between a group of teacher educators. Our discussions – generated in an explicit attempt to pin down the elusive 'evenmoreness' – provide the analytical material for this chapter. Alongside the group conversations are two unstructured interviews undertaken in one instance some months before and in the other some months after the group discussion. All of these conversations are undertaken with colleagues who might reasonably be described as working friends.

My own teacher educator voice is embedded within these discussions.

In engaging with my colleagues in a research enterprise, not only am I engaged with the world I study, I am simultaneously both an insider and outsider: I am part of the world I study while being positioned in a very specific space in relation to that world. We are all Higher Education (HE) practitioners but our terms and conditions of service do not reflect this commonality. My role as academic contact carries particular affordances and obligations in terms of scholarly activity, teaching responsibilities and support for research. In view of our evenmore conversations I am, in one moment a PCE TEd, and in the next a co-researcher generating data for analysis.

The chapter contributes towards the development of our theoretical understanding of broader social phenomenon – namely teacher educators' pedagogic being: a being that implies something more than knowing about and passing on how to teach, a being that is indeed quite distinct; a being that implies *evenmore* than being a good teacher.

They [college teachers] can't [teach teachers how to teach], they miss some of the key things. They're not well versed enough in learning theories and what-have-you – it's something they did on their CertEd that wasn't important, rather than we who live and breathe our pedagogy.

(Programme leader (1), College A)

Through and from this methodology I draw towards a conclusion that if there is a distinct pedagogy associated with PCE teacher education, a definable evenmoreness, it is that PCE TEds *are* what we teach. When our distinct evenmoreness is heard – it is heard as embodied and enacted.

Critical question

> What is the difference between being and becoming a teacher educator?

How different does being a PCE teacher educator [as opposed to a PCE teacher] feel, does it feel very different – do you think?

(Programme leader, College B)

While all those present were able to quote some years' experience as a teacher, the shift from teacher to teacher educator was a decisive one. Becoming a teacher educator was not the fulfilment of a long-held desire. Indeed, the experiences of becoming a teacher educator '*by accident*' resonated for all of us,

I got a phone call [from the Teacher Education Programme Manager] saying there's a job coming up, would you like to apply? We think you would be good at this!

(Programme leader (2), College C)

There is, as Murray and Male (2005) argue, a substantive difference between being employed in the post of teacher educator and assuming teacher educator as a professional identity. They suggest – being and feeling – as two distinct states; it is therefore possible *to be* a teacher educator without actually *feeling* like one. Despite successful careers in teaching, the 28 HE-based teacher educators who participated in the Murray and Male (2005) study took between two and three years to fully inhabit their new professional identities. This disjuncture between being a teacher educator and actually feeling like a teacher educator rests upon Southworth's (2002) parallel disjuncture between a situational self and a substantial self. The situational self is determined by interaction with others; it is a contextual, contingent and transient self – that rests upon the actuality of being. The substantial self is a more enduring long-term project less amenable to change. It is a feeling, dispositional self. The transition from PCE teacher to teacher educator is complete when these two distinct selves (situational and substantive) become aligned.

That Murray and Male (2005) base their study on the experiences of school teacher educators is significant; two of the defining characteristics that constitute a teacher educator's substantive self are developing the pedagogic knowledge required for working with HE (ie adult) students rather than children and developing a research profile (Murray and Male, 2005, p 126). Neither of these considerations are resonant with the PCE practitioner who becomes a teacher educator on the basis of their substantive experience of pedagogies suitable for working with adults – sometimes in the context of HE (in FE) provision. While the research-active profile sits somewhat askance for the novice teacher educator scholar, for PCE TEds something more fundamental is at stake. Our terms and conditions of service do not allow working space for scholarship. '*HE in FE teachers, although wishing to undertake research, are not given time to do so by management, as they [management] do not see research as a priority*' (Feather, 2012, p 246).

Employed by FE institutions who offer HE provision, FE-based teacher educators typically teach the same number of hours (750 to 950 annually) as their FE colleagues. There is no meaningful institutional space for them to acquaint themselves with emerging policy and research let alone develop a research profile. My suggestion here is that while developing a research profile is a desirable feature for the PCE TEd, it is unlikely to be a defining characteristic for those working in FE institutions.

I think that I don't quite see myself as a HE practitioner because I don't have the supported time to research; however, reading around current research has helped me to feel more like a teacher educator.

(Programme leader (2), College C)

While there is a clear basis for suggesting that it may take some years to fully feel confident in the role of a teacher educator – whatever feelings might shape the professional disposition – it is the actuality of being a teacher educator that interests me most here, especially being a teacher educator, whatever feelings might surround it. One practitioner describes the shift from teacher to teacher educator and the associated feelings.

I had a journey from one place to another place some miles away. I left an FE college on the Friday and started at the university centre on the Monday, and [...] then I just had to do it. I had to be that teacher educator from day one, so there was no sense of this slow evolution from being one thing to being another thing. I became that thing overnight.

(Programme leader, College B)

The first few moments of teacher educator being can challenge a secure sense of professional self:

When I first got here it was quite odd being in a room knowing that last week I was in an FE college, today here I am at the university centre and people are calling me up and expecting things from me, asking me for advice about stuff that I have to say I didn't have a clue about ... it took me ages to get my head around this stuff ... I thought this is the most bizarre thing, what is this?

(Programme leader, College B)

This is not to undermine the value of exploring teacher educator becoming. It is however important to recognise that identity – including professional identity – is always and already a becoming. I am suggesting that developing, establishing and maintaining a professional identity as a teacher educator is an ongoing process. When the notion or experience of becoming a teacher educator is discussed in the literature, it too frequently implies that it is possible to identify a specific moment (indeed Murray and Male (2005) empirically identify that moment) when one stops becoming a teacher educator and finally becomes one – as a distinct state of being. In talking about teacher educator being, I accept its inherent fluidity. This allows me to make sense of the feeling that:

You need to be at the forefront of every new government agenda so that we can take that into our classrooms and so that our new trainees can be aware of it whereas if you're a lecturer in whichever bit of FE then you don't actually have to be bothered, you just wait 'til someone tells you such and such a training is available and yeah, oh this is what you now need to know, so that's sort of filtered down through a management structure whereas we need to know it at the same time as that management structure, so you're almost like doing that role as well. Sometimes before.

(Programme leader, College D)

This sounds to me like a distinct sense of pride in being able to manage the risk, uncertainty and doubt that goes along with the ever-changing policy landscape of PCE practice. In this landscape, our situational selves are in a perpetual state of flux. What we are required to do, to believe, to teach and to embody have few points of anchorage. The teacher educators' being is a fluid being. But, it is a fluid 'being' rather than a static 'becoming'.

Critical question

➢ What is the difference between teacher education as modelling and teacher education embodying?

Teacher educators are required to model that which they teach. In developing the pedagogy of our trainees modelling takes places on two levels. There is an explicit modelling in as much as we show students what to do in the classroom, by doing it. We use creative and innovative teaching methods that can be adopted and adapted across different curricular subjects.

(Programme leader, College B)

There is however another step required which is further, higher or deeper than this; a step that might be considered controversially as triple loop learning or '*deutero-learning*' (Tosey et al, 2011), an approach to learning defined by critical reflexivity and collective mindfulness. Teacher educators are required to stand reflexively outside themselves in order to articulate their understanding of their own professionalism.

After an observation, I really want one of my students to question, 'Well who gives you the right to tell me to do that or to look at that?' and I think, 'Well somebody needs to do it.' I question that type of thing ... and I'm waiting for one of my students to question why I've got the right to judge them ...

(Programme leader, College C)

The PCE TEd moves comfortably between levels and loops of learning, from the question 'Are we doing things right?' (single loop) to the more reflective 'Are we doing the right thing?' (double loop) and standing outside both of these to the critically reflexive '*On what basis do we make well-informed choices regarding what to do?*' (Romme and Van Witteloostuijn, 1999, p 452). As Loughran and Berry (2005) point out, beyond a pedagogy based on transmission, there is modelling. In this chapter I suggest that, beyond a pedagogy based on modelling, there is pedagogic embodiment. An embodiment that offers trainees insight into the pedagogic being: how to reason, feel, think and act like a pedagogue. This is an embodied and enacted pedagogy. Accepting that our professional identities are a fluctuating composite of what we feel and what we think others feel about us, the PCE TEd articulates this sense of professional self:

[Being a teacher educator] *doesn't feel different* [to being an FE or HE teacher] *because you're teaching, but I think it's the expectations your trainees place on you. I don't think students necessarily see university lecturers as teachers, whereas they see us as teachers because we're teaching on a teacher training course.*

(Programme leader, College D)

There are then additional expectations that students seem to have of their teacher educators that were not the same as those expected of either FE teachers or HE lecturers, and while we are not fully defined by those expectations, they are part of the professional landscape and thus something we have to negotiate. For some teacher educators this meant an ongoing relationship in which the role of tutor, mentor, manager and friend was fused.

So an embodied pedagogy is more or other than modelling; more or other than critical reflexivity. Moreover, the modelling we do is even more than modelling actual PCE practice. Our trainees are learning to teach adult students in FE; PCE TEds are teaching HE students who will become critical practitioners. In other words, the audiences – the purpose of our pedagogy – are different. What works and what is appropriate is different, critical reflexivity makes these dis/connections explicit. Working in HE you're not bound by FE restrictions on what good teaching should be, the more prescriptive elements of it. I don't feel that I'm bound by the really silly things that you have to do in FE.

(Programme leader, College B)

It's a dilemma ... teaching trainees to teach in a way that we don't necessarily feel committed to.

(Programme leader (2), College C)

The PCE TEd models 'being excellent to the nth degree'.

(Programme leader, College D)

IN A **NUTSHELL**

I have explored the *evenmoreness* of PCE TEds using collaborative auto-ethnography. This methodology seems best suited to breaking through the scholarly silence that surrounds this occupational group. By paying close attention to teacher educator being rather than teacher educator becoming, I identify an embodied critical reflexivity implied by the sentiment 'we are what we teach' as a distinct and defining characteristic of PCE TEd pedagogy. This embodied critical reflexivity acknowledges experience, context and a commitment to being excellent to the nth degree.

REFLECTIONS ON **CRITICAL ISSUES**

This chapter explores what if anything distinguishes being a teacher in PCE from being a teacher educator in PCE. Having accepted the challenge of pinning down the elusive 'evenmoreness' of teacher educator being, I have mapped a distinct teacher educator being as enacted and embodied. Using hybrid methodologies – collective auto-ethnography and interviews, the chapter crafts the voices of PCE TEds to illustrate what it is to enact and to embody a space surrounded by scholarly silence. These voices emphasise teacher educator being rather than teacher educator becoming, and gesture towards where and how the PCE TEds' 'evenmoreness' might be understood. The PCE TEds' pedagogic being is enacted and embodied, standing in stark contrast to both FE teaching and HE lecturing.

REFERENCES

Ball, S J (1990) *Politics and Policy Making in Education: Explorations in Policy Sociology*. New York: Routledge.

Crawley, J (2013) Endless Patience and a Strong Belief in What Makes a Good Teacher: Teacher Educators in Post-Compulsory Education in England and Their Professional Situation. *Research in Post-Compulsory Education*, 18: 336–47.

Dennis, C A (2015) Locating Post-16 Professionalism: Public Spaces as Dissenting Spaces. *Research in Post-Compulsory Education*, 20: 64–77.

Feather, D (2012) Oh to Be a Scholar – an HE in FE Perspective. *Journal of Further and Higher Education*, 36: 243–61.

Korthagen, F A J (1995) A Reflection on Five Reflective Accounts. Theme Issue Self-study and Living Educational Theory. *Teacher Education Quarterly*, 22: 99–105.

Loughran, J and Berry, A (2005) Modelling by Teacher Educators. *Teaching and Teacher Education*, 21: 193–203.

Morley, L and Rasool, N (2000) School Effectiveness: New Managerialism, Quality and the Japanization of Education. *Journal of Education Policy*, 15: 169–83.

Murray, J and Male, T (2005) Becoming a Teacher Educator: Evidence from the Field. *Teaching and Teacher Education*, 21: 125–42.

Romme, A G L and van Witteloostuijn, A (1999) Circular Organizing and Triple Loop Learning. *Journal of Organizational Change Management*, 12: 439–54.

Southworth, G (2002) *Looking into Primary Headship: A Research Based Interpretation*. London: Routledge.

Swennen, A and Bates, T (2010) The Professional Development of Teacher Educators. *Professional Development in Education*, 36: 1–7.

Tosey, P, Visser, M and Saunders, M N (2011) The Origins and Conceptualizations of 'Triple-loop' Learning: A Critical Review. *Management Learning*, 43: 291–307.

CRITICAL **ISSUES**

- *What defines the post compulsory sector?*
- *Who and what is the sector for?*
- *How might the sector look in the future?*

Why is the post compulsory education sector so hard to define?

'... *everything that does not happen in schools or universities*' (Kennedy, 1997, p 1) is the 'throwaway definition' for the sector that begins the influential Learning Works report to the government on widening participation in further education (FE) published in 1997, usually referred to as the Kennedy Report. This description has been frequently used since, though it is not strictly accurate. Colleges in England taught 24,000 14- and 15-year-olds in 2015 (AoC, 2015, p 14) and around ten per cent of all higher education in England is college-based; the proportion is higher in Scotland. No wonder that Kennedy herself added that to exhaustively define the sector '*would be God's own challenge because it is such a large and fertile section of the education world*' (1997, p 1). Even the name of the sector is disputed. FE; learning and skills; lifelong learning; vocational education and training, are all terms in common use. The one adopted for this book, post compulsory education (PCE), is current even if it does not reflect the change in legislation to make 18 the statutory minimum age to leave education and training. The majority of teaching in colleges is for young people aged 16 to 18 and so is compulsory. Nonetheless, PCE has retained a meaning, especially for teacher education designed for teachers outside schools who are no longer legally required to be qualified. So, why is the sector, this filling in the educational sandwich, so difficult to define that the simplest explanation is to say what it does not do? This chapter attempts to answer that question by asking a series of key questions. We start by considering the students.

Who is PCE for?

The problem with defining the PCE sector is the very diversity of its provision and its students:

» mainly vocational but with significant academic provision;

» mainly for 16- to 19-year-olds but with substantial numbers of older adults;

» funded nationally but with distinctive local differences.

Although the sector has been termed the *'neglected middle child'* of education, squeezed between schools and universities (Foster, 2005, p 58), PCE is certainly not a numerically marginal element of the education system. FE colleges educate and train 2.9 million people in England. There are 773,000 16- to 18-year-olds who study in colleges, compared with 442,000 in schools. A further 71,000 16- to 18-year-olds undertake apprenticeships through colleges and two million adults study or train in English colleges (AoC, 2015). The most common metaphor for the sector is that of Cinderella, which has been used at least since 1935 to describe *'the technical side of education'* in Britain (Petrie, 2015, p 2). This image of a drearily passive sector waiting for a prince to arrive has recently been challenged (Daley et al, 2015), but the prevalence of the fairy-tale metaphor is indicative of PCE being overlooked or at least misunderstood, especially by policymakers. Hodgson et al (2015, p 1) argue that the sector is *'for other people's children'*. Few policymakers associated with any recent government have had direct experience of PCE as they and their children are most likely to have followed academic routes through school sixth forms, many in private schools. That lack of direct experience or knowledge has not stopped politicians from tinkering with the sector over the past two decades and for that reason Keep (2006, p 47) has described policymaking on education and skills in Britain as *'Playing with the Biggest Trainset in the World'*. This attitude is also a question of social class. The education system in Britain reflects the inequalities of British society, so while many middle-class children do attend colleges, the sector has lower cultural status than other sectors of education, such as universities, and students in PCE are mainly working class (Avis, 2009).

What does the sector look like?

There are in England alone (Ofsted, 2015, p 7) 230 general FE colleges, 94 sixth form colleges, 55 independent specialist colleges, 428 independent learning providers and further provision in prisons and adult education institutions. This is, therefore, a large and varied sector where making generalisations is problematic. To compound that problem there is, moreover, far less systematically collected data on PCE in Britain than there is for schools or higher education and there is virtually none on private training providers. This is probably also indicative of PCE's lowly status by comparison with schools and universities.

A general FE college?

Using data provided by a sample of colleges, the Education and Training Foundation (ETF) tentatively described a typical General Further Education College (GFEC) in England in 2012–13 (ETF, 2014, p 10) as well as providing a statistical overview of the whole sector in England in 2013–14 (ETF, 2015), some of which is shown below in Table 3.1.

Table 3.1 General Further Education Colleges in England

Expenditure of the average college in 2012–13	£21m
Number of students in the average college in 2012–13	5574 (many part time)
Number of teachers in the average college in 2012–13	307 (many part time)
Proportion of contracts for teaching staff in 2013–14	48.7%
Proportion of women working in colleges in 2013–14	63%
Proportion of staff under the age of 40 in 2013–14	30%
Proportion of part-time teaching staff in 2013–14	62.3%
Median pay of teachers in 2013–14	£31,000 to £31,999
Turnover of teaching staff in 2013–14	15.9%

Source: ETF (2014, p 10; 2015, pp 25–39).

All of these are carefully calculated statistics but we need to treat them with caution because, as ETF make clear in their annual reports, they are based on a small number of returns; around a third of colleges in 2012–13 and even fewer the following year (ETF 2015, p 5). More than that, though, reducing such a diverse sector to average figures risks misrepresentation and that is just for England. Colleges and other providers, even in the same regions, can be quite different in size and focus. There are several large colleges in rural settings with a focus on land-based industries; some colleges offer a large range of higher education courses; many independent training providers are very small but some have a wider regional or even national reach. PCE institutions are as diverse as the sector, even though many share similar traits. One claim often made by PCE institutions is that they reflect their local economy and they direct their courses to the particular needs of their local employers. With the greater regionalisation of FE in England, discussed in the following subsection, that claim may be harder to justify.

Regionalisation

Regionalisation is still only nascent in England, but is more established elsewhere in the UK. In Northern Ireland, Scotland and Wales, colleges have been encouraged and required to organise their provision regionally for some time. PCE is a policy-led sector and in the devolved education systems within the UK, PCE or its equivalents in Northern Ireland, Scotland and Wales are increasingly distinctive. In England, public funding for colleges comes from the Department for Education for students aged 16–19 and from the Skills Funding Agency for students over 19, and inspections are carried out by Ofsted. Each of the other nations has their own funding system as well as their own inspectorate. As Hodgson et al (2015, pp 7–8) note, because of their smaller populations (that of Northern Ireland is considerably less than Greater Manchester) and because of broadly social democratic rather than neoliberal policies, education professionals in the smaller nations have much greater influence on policymaking than in England. Indeed, Hodgson et al (p 12) conclude that 'England is increasingly becoming an outlier' as a result of neoliberal policies even if the PCE sectors of all four UK nations appear similar by comparison with the rest of Europe.

Major differences between the four nations' PCE sectors are also apparent in higher education provided in further education colleges (HE in FE). Colleges throughout the UK have provided HE courses for decades but the proportions now differ significantly. In England around 8 per cent of HE is college based; in Wales it is 1.4 per cent; in Scotland and Northern Ireland 18 per cent is college based. Again, generalisation across institutions can be misleading. In 2010–11, for example, of the 17,445 first degree entrants (part time and full time) in all English FE colleges, over 3000 went to just three FE institutions, while the majority of colleges had fewer than 100 such students. Similarly, many HE courses in colleges lead to qualifications other than full degrees, such as foundation degrees and Higher National Diplomas. More generally, though, most of the sector's HE provision is vocational, such as courses in childcare; and most HE in FE students are part time, a very clear distinction from university-based HE which is overwhelmingly full time and increasingly so (see Avis and Orr, 2016).

HE in FE has attracted the attention of some policymakers. Following the findings of the Dearing Report on Higher Education, the New Labour government (1997–2005) specifically promoted HE in FE as a vehicle for both social mobility and enhancing the skills of the UK's workforce. Though less of a priority under the Coalition (2005–2010) or current Conservative government, HE in FE is still identified as central to policies around widening participation (WP) in HE and to skills development. These two intertwined elements, social and economic, are crucial to understanding the specific purpose of HE in FE (at least for certain policymakers) but also of the PCE sector more generally.

What is the PCE sector for?

In the three decades up to the 2015 election there had been 61 Secretaries of State responsible for skills policy in Britain. Between them they produced 13 major Acts of Parliament, and skills policy had flipped between government departments or been shared between departments on ten different occasions (City and Guilds, 2014, p 1). That level of political instability makes long-term planning in the sector impossible but even within this political uncertainty recurring tropes in policy are apparent. In 2005 Bill Rammell, then British minister of state for Higher Education and Lifelong Learning stated that (LSC, 2005, p 1) 'Further Education is the engine room for skills and social justice in this country'. The following year the Leitch Review of Skills asserted *'where skills were once **a** key driver of prosperity and fairness, they are now **the** key driver'* (Leitch, 2006, p 46).

These statements were typical of the New Labour period, which saw colleges funding increase greatly alongside much greater scrutiny and control. A statutory requirement for teachers in FE to be teacher qualified was introduced by New Labour, demonstrating the importance placed on the whole sector at the time. Though this requirement was rescinded by the Coalition government there is continuity between the policies of recent UK governments, even if their statements on the importance of the sector are not so forthright. There is still the frequent conflation of skills and social justice, as well as the association of participation in education (most especially HE) with social mobility. Above all, there is still emphasis on the supply side of skills for the nation's workforce rather than on how the demands for skills might be managed or on how skills are deployed in workplaces. Nevertheless, and despite the occasionally high-blown rhetoric, the point remains that the primary function of the sector is to provide education and training that is about or for work. The final report of the government's Commission on Adult Vocational Teaching and Learning (CAVTL) published in 2013 also emphasises the need for:

high quality vocational education and training (VET) that can respond to and prepare us all for changes in work, advances in knowledge and technology, and the increasing demand for people with higher levels of skill.

(CAVTL, 2013, p 7)

The PCE sector addresses these needs and it does so despite much poorer funding than that for other sectors of education. The CAVTL Report and subsequent publications are more nuanced and cautious than many government pronouncements on the sector, which can lose sight of the individual in generic discussion of 'up-skilling' and social mobility.

For the individual, PCE is very often the home of the second chance at education and training. Participation may well be associated with gaining better or more worthwhile employment, but it may also relate to a personal sense of fulfilment. Access to HE courses for adults exemplify this well but PCE changes individual lives in many ways, which makes working in the sector very rewarding. This is also why having qualified teachers is important, because what those teachers do is important for their individual students. But is the sector genuinely able to improve the skills of the nation's workforce or enhance social mobility? British governments have been keen to promote and even quantify social mobility, which the Cabinet Office defines as 'a measure of how free people are to improve their position in society' (Cabinet Office, 2011, p 15). This concept of social mobility is, though, narrowly individualistic and ignores structural inequalities related to race, class and gender. While the relative upward mobility of individuals is implied, the commensurate and necessary relative downward mobility of other individuals is disregarded. Even if we accept this narrow and individualistic definition of social mobility, there is little evidence to suggest that access to education through PCE automatically leads to relative upward movement. Certainly, policies to widen participation in higher education (including HE in FE) have been enormously successful. More young people and especially more young people from modest backgrounds are attending FE and HE than ever before, which is to be warmly welcomed

(AoC, 2016; BIS, 2015). But that is not the same as relative social mobility, let alone social justice. Full-time degree graduates who studied at colleges are on average more likely to be unemployed and earning less six months after graduation. They are also less likely to continue onto further courses than their equivalents who studied at universities (HEFCE, 2013, p 11). We may reasonably surmise that part-time adult students in colleges, for whom national data is not systematically collected, fare better than their younger full-time colleagues. Nevertheless, simply attending college or achieving qualifications does not necessarily lead to the relative social mobility that governments have desired. To ask PCE to compensate for or even alleviate deep-seated social and economic inequalities is to ask too much. That is not, though, to deny the transformative power of PCE for many people who have benefitted greatly from their involvement. As Avis and Orr (2016) have argued elsewhere, education such as that offered in the PCE sector may not change society, but it might change lives.

Looking to the future of the sector: how is PCE changing?

PCE is currently undergoing major upheaval throughout the UK and especially in England. According to Keep (2014, p 3), '*The old model of English/UK skills policy is rapidly fading away, and a new world is being born*'. The reason for this transformation of the sector, Keep explains, is the political decision to make radical cuts in funding for PCE as part of the government's programme of spending reductions. Spending per student on vocational courses in the sector was already well below that for students on three-year HE courses (Wolf, 2015, p 66). Yet, while policymakers may previously have tinkered with the sector, these most recent policies threaten the very existence of many PCE organisations, which could merge or close. The move to greater regionalisation is one vehicle for this kind of rationalisation or reduction of provision although that possible shrinkage of the sector's institutions does not inevitably mean fewer students. Less public funding may also have other structural effects. The government has argued that investment in training from employers will take the place of public funding, though there is little evidence that this has occurred. The regulation of public funding has, however, been a very powerful lever for the implementation of policy and the diminishing power of that lever may reduce the control central government has over PCE. That may in turn lead to what Keep (2014, p 10) has called '*a more distributed model of power*' in the sector with more local decision-making, but also more instability. In any case, the sector will look different in five years.

IN A **NUTSHELL**

The PCE sector is susceptible to shifts in policy, so in order to cope and thrive, teacher education and TEds need to manage constant change while maintaining a commitment in their practice to their own professional values. Perhaps the more the sector changes, the more it remains the same thing: a sector focussed on vocational education and training. Interestingly, Tummons (2014) has described how little the teacher education curriculum was altered through the introduction of centralised standards. Nevertheless, being forewarned of shifts in policy can allow collective campaigns to be mounted, such as that which successfully prevented cuts in English as a Second or Other Language (ESOL) provision in 2011 (Peutrell, 2015), and being forewarned can also allow individual teachers to prepare or adapt. At the very least, teachers need to know that what they are doing today is unlikely to be exactly what they will be doing in five years.

REFLECTIONS ON **CRITICAL ISSUES**

PCE is so large and diverse that it is difficult to describe succinctly, which means that it is very often defined by what it is not. The majority of work-related education and training courses in the UK does however take place in PCE. Despite its size and importance most policymakers overlook the sector but it quickly becomes indispensable when they need to implement policy on skills. Young people at colleges also tend to come from less advantaged backgrounds than those who attend, for example, school sixth forms, but there are very significant regional and national differences in provision and attendance across the UK. For two decades PCE has been constantly in a state of transition, at the whim of whichever politician is briefly in charge at any given time. Recently, PCE has also endured very significant cuts in funding. In all four nations of the UK the PCE sector of the future is likely to include fewer but larger colleges, which focus more and more exclusively on vocational courses.

REFERENCES

AoC (Association of Colleges) (2015) *College Key Facts 2014–2015*. London: AoC.

AoC (Association of Colleges) (2016) *College Key Facts 2015–2016*. London: AoC.

Avis, J (2009) *Education, Policy and Social Justice: Learning and Skills*. London: Continuum.

Avis, J and Orr, K (2016) HE in FE: Vocationalism, Class and Social Justice. *Research in Post-Compulsory Education*, 21: 49–65.

BIS (Department for Business, Innovation and Skills) (2015) *Statistical First Release: Participation Rates in Higher Education: Academic Years 2006/7–2013/14 (Provisional)*. London: BIS.

Cabinet Office (2015) *Opening Doors, Breaking Barriers: A Strategy for Social Mobility*. London: Cabinet Office.

CAVTL (Commission on Adult Vocational Teaching and Learning) (2013) *It's About Work: Excellent Adult Vocational Teaching and Learning*. London: Learning and Skills Improvement Service (LSIS).

City and Guilds (2014) *Sense and Instability: Three Decades of Skills and Employment Policy*. London: City and Guilds.

Daley, M, Orr, K and Petrie, J (eds) (2015) *Further Education and the Twelve Dancing Princesses*. London: IOE Press.

ETF (Education and Training Foundation) (2014) *Further Education Workforce Data for England: Analysis of the 2012–13 Staff Individualised Record (SIR) Data*. London: ETF.

ETF (Education and Training Foundation) (2015) *Further Education Workforce Data for England: Analysis of the 2013–2014 Staff Individualised Record (SIR) Data*. London: ETF.

Foster, A (2005) *Realising the Potential: A Review of the Future Role of Further Education Colleges*. London: DfES.

HEFCE (Higher Education Funding Council for England) (2013) *Destinations of Leavers from Higher Education in Further Education Colleges: Key Findings: Leavers up to Academic Year 2010–11*. Bristol: HEFCE.

Hodgson, A, Bailey, B and Lucas, N (2015) What Is FE? in Hodgson, A (ed) *The Coming of Age for FE? Reflections on the Past and Future Role of Further Education Colleges in England*. London: IOE Press, pp 1–23.

Keep, E (2006) State Control of the English Education and Training System: Playing with the Biggest Trainset in the World. *Journal of Vocational Education and Training*, 58: 47–64.

Keep, E (2014) *What Does Skills Policy Look Like Now the Money Has Run Out?* London: Association of Colleges.

Kennedy, H (1997) *Learning Works: Widening Participation in Further Education*. Coventry: Further Education Funding Council.

LSC (Learning and Skills Council) (2005) *Learning and Skills – the Agenda for Change: The Prospectus*. Coventry: LSC.

Leitch, S (2006) *Prosperity for All in the Global Economy: World Class Skills, Final Report*. London: The Stationery Office.

Ofsted (2015) *The Annual Report of Her Majesty's Chief Inspector of Education, Children's Services and Skills 2014/15*. London: Ofsted.

Petrie, J (2015) Introduction: How Grimm Is FE? in Daly, M, Orr, K and Petrie, J (eds) *Further Education and the Twelve Dancing Princesses*. London: IOE Press, pp 1–12.

Peutrell, R (2015) Action for ESOL: Pedagogy, Professionalism and Politics, in Daly, M, Orr, K and Petrie, J (eds) *Further Education and the Twelve Dancing Princesses*. London: IOE Press, pp 139–56.

Tummons, J (2014) Professional Standards in Teacher Education: Tracing Discourses of Professionalism through the Analysis of Textbooks. *Research in Post-Compulsory Education*, 19: 417–32.

Wolf, A (2015) *Issues and Ideas, Heading for the Precipice: Can Further and Higher Education Funding Policies Be Sustained?* Report for the Policy Institute at King's College London. London: Policy Institute.

Lynn Machin

CRITICAL **ISSUES**

- *Why has the post compulsory education (PCE) sector been the subject of constant changes?*

- *What have these changes been?*

- *Why is an understanding of the history and development of PCE and initial teacher education important?*

A policy-driven sector

Critical question

➣ What changes are you anticipating in teacher education within the forthcoming year?

Your answer to this question may have included changes to how teacher training is inspected, new regulations, an increase or decrease in the number of trainees enrolling onto teacher training programmes or many other possibilities. A shifting landscape in PCE is not new and as Orr outlines in Chapter 3, is shaped by social, political and economic considerations and the visions of successive governments of a sector which can equip learners with the skills necessary to work in a global economy.

This chapter spotlights significant policies, reports and Acts since 1944 (listed in Table 4.1), prior to which little information about the PCE sector exists (Lucas, 2004). The Butler Act (1944), while not directly related to teacher education in PCE, was pivotal for its introduction of free education and the raising of the school leaving age to 15. In this sense it was a platform for other reports that were more closely associated with PCE. The McNair Report (1944) swiftly followed on from Butler and outlined deficiencies in an existing system of training teachers that centred round apprenticeship models which had little, if any, theoretical input (Lucas, 2004, p 1). In the late 1990s a flood of other reports, policies and Acts were produced (Table 4.1). These have all shaped current PCE teacher education provision.

Table 4.1 PCE reports, policies and Acts

Date	Title	Comments
1944	Butler Act	Introduced a tripartite system of secondary education, ie grammar, secondary modern and technical schools.
1944	McNair Report	Raised concerns about deficiencies in the recruitment and training of teachers, particularly those in PCE.
1957	Willis Jackson Report	Promoted the concept of a qualified post compulsory workforce.
1966	Russell Report	Continued to build on the concept of a qualified post compulsory workforce.
1972	James Report	Promoted PCE teacher education accredited by universities.
1992	Further and Higher Education Act	Transferred responsibility of funding and governing PCE from LEAs to the Further Education Funding Council (FEFC).
1998	Further Education National Training Organisation	FENTO produced a set of national teaching standards in 2001. Awarding bodies and universities reviewed their provision using these standards. Although sporadic, training of teachers increased.
2002	Success for All Report	The first of several reports recommending that PCE teacher education be reviewed and that properly trained teachers could improve the UK's workforce and economic prospects.
2003	The Initial Teacher Education of Further Education Teachers	Concluded that FENTO provided a good baseline of what was required of teachers but lacked any ethos of professional development.
2004	Equipping our Teachers for the Future	Pivotal in the creation of Lifelong Learning UK and the introduction of new ITE awards. This report argued that training beyond qualified teaching status was necessary in order for teachers to meet their learners' needs.

Table 4.1 (*cont.*)

Date	Title	Comments
2005	Foster Report, Realising the Potential	Emphasised the need to address the issues of an ageing workforce and to improve vocational and pedagogic skills through comprehensive workforce planning.
2006	Raising Skills, Improving Life Chances	Considered that the UK's economic future depended on productivity as a nation and that PCE providers were central to achieving a high skills economy, but were not yet achieving that goal.
2007	Lifelong Learning UK (LLUK) standards	Replaced the FENTO standards
2007	The Further Education Teachers' Qualifications Regulations	Required all teachers working in PCE to be registered with the Institute for Learning (IfL) and submit evidence of qualification and annual CPD. All lecturers joining the sector after 2001 needed to become qualified within their identified role. The status of Qualified Teacher Learning and Skills (QTLS) for qualified PCE teachers was also introduced.
2009	Enquiry into Teacher Training in Vocational Education	Focussed on whether teachers in PCE were being trained in the skills to deliver the emerging 14–19 vocational curricula. It also proposed the merger of the General Teaching Council (GTC) and the IfL so that those working within PCE would have parity of qualifications with school teachers.
2009	Skills for Growth	Proposed phasing out funding for the IfL and the membership fee payable by trainees and teachers.
2011	Wolf Report	Considered how vocational education for 14- to 19-year-olds could be improved and promoted the concept of PCE teaching in schools to ensure that learners were taught by those best suited to do so.
2012	Lingfield Report	Recommended the de-regulation of teacher education and suggested that the 2007 regulations had not had the intended impact.
2012	Business, Innovation and Skills (BIS)	Following consultations BIS countered Lingfield's proposed revocation of regulated teacher education.

Table 4.1 (*cont.*)

Date	Title	Comments
2013	Learning and Skills Improvement Service (LSIS)	LSIS introduced a new framework of units and credits for ITE.
2014	The Education and Training Foundation	The ETF sets professional standards, codes of behaviour and develops qualifications.
2015	The Society for Education and Training (SET)	The SET provides a professional body for teachers within PCE.

Critical question

➣ Which of the policies, reports and Acts in Table 4.1 have had a direct impact on the PCE teacher education provision delivered at your organisation and why?

Early approaches to initial teacher education in PCE

Taking a leap forward from McNair's Report (1944) to a time when (under a Conservative government) unemployment hit an all-time high, miners were striking and Margaret Thatcher was the Secretary for State for Education, the James Report (1972) emerged. Lord James emphasised the need for PCE teacher education and suggested that higher education institutions (HEIs), as well as the awarding organisations (eg City and Guilds, Edexcel), should accredit teacher education and strengthen their links with colleges. Subsequently, HEIs created several awards, for example, a level 7 Post Graduate Certificate in Education and a level 4 or 5 Certificate in Education. Awarding bodies often accredited introductory, lower academic level (eg levels 3 and 4) shorter courses than those delivered by the HEIs.

There was disparity in how these awards were delivered. As with the earlier apprenticeship models of teacher training noted in the McNair Report (1944) the awards delivered by the awarding bodies tended to be less theoretical than those delivered by the HEIs. What all awards had in common was that they were mostly delivered to in-service trainees and focussed on subject pedagogical competence (IfL, 2006).

Teaching in PCE was (and still is), for many, a second career. Many teachers also worked full or part time in industry doing jobs relating to their occupational craft. While the time constraints of doing more than one job would have influenced teachers' decisions about training it is also likely that '*few teachers embraced the opportunity or provision of any training offered to them*' due to an allegiance with their craft more than their pedagogical development, thereby reducing the '*impact that initial teacher education could have for teachers*' (Robson, 1998, p 585).

On the basis of claims that it would increase efficiency, the (Conservative) government passed the Further and Higher Education Act (April 1992), removed funding and governing PCE from the control of local education authorities (LEAs) to the Further Education Funding Council (FEFC); the latter becoming the Learning Skills Council in 2000 (Armitage et al, 2003) and then the Skills Funding Agency (SFA) in April 2010. Managed by a board of governors and senior management, colleges were able to act with a good degree of independence according to Smithers and Robinson (2000). However, they still needed to adhere to national strategies and not all colleges managed to do this; thereby falling short of the '*standards that were acceptable to the Government or funding authorities*' (Tight, 2002, p 139). Rather than being released from government intervention, PCE continued to be the target of reports and Acts (Table 4.1), all of which recommended improvement to teacher education and the raising of standards (Lucas, 2004, p 35).

Changes to the sector came quickly and a sector that, when compared with compulsory sector, had previously been labelled as the '*Cinderella*' sector (Randle and Brady, 1997, p 121) became the focus of the (then) Labour government's attention. During Labour's time in office (1997–2010) several reports (Table 4.1.) determined that quality PCE teaching provision was necessary for the development of '*a world leading education system*' that would be at the '*heart of national priorities for economy and society*' (DIUS, 2007, p 2) and that '*high quality post-16 provision*' was necessary to '*meet the requirements of employers, individuals and communities*' (DfES, 1999, p 23). With this in mind, David Blunkett, the then Secretary of State for Education and Employment, issued a Green Paper, The Learning Age (DfEE, 1998), which recommended the implementation of a Further Education National Training Organisation (FENTO) to oversee and endorse teacher education qualifications.

Critical question

➤ What is your view about PCE having a regulatory body for teacher training qualifications?

Teaching standards

In 1999, FENTO introduced a set of teaching standards and in 2001 regulations were introduced '*compelling all lecturers to gain a nationally recognised qualification*' (Lingfield, 2012, p 12) that would be underpinned by the FENTO standards. These occupational standards adopted a similar, codifiable criteria approach to that used for National Vocational Qualifications focussing on roles and functions (Lester, 2014, p 2). With more than 300 descriptors, they were described by Nasta (2009, p 5) as '*staggering*'. Lucas (2004, p 36) maintained that these standards were open to interpretation and did not reflect the diversity of PCE as the design and delivery of initial teacher education '*varied enormously*'.

Perhaps unsurprisingly many teachers chose not to avail themselves of the opportunities presented to them to become qualified (Lucas, 2004).

A report from Ofsted concluded that the FENTO standards provided a good baseline of what was required of teachers but lacked any ethos of professional development (Ofsted, 2003). Consequently, in 2005, FENTO was replaced by Lifelong Learning UK (LLUK). As a sector skills council (SSC) LLUK had a remit to work in partnership across the UK to create conditions for increased employer investment in skills and use this to create jobs and sustainable economic growth. Alongside LLUK was a subsidiary organisation, Standards Verification UK (SVUK), which approved PCE teacher training qualifications (Lingfield, 2012, p 13). Together with these new bodies came Centres of Excellence in Teacher Training (CETTs), Centres of Vocational Excellence (CoVEs), the Learning and Skills Council (LSC) and the sector's professional body, the Institute for Learning (IfL).

PCE in the twenty-first century

Lifelong Learning UK (LLUK)

Around the same time as the demise of FENTO and the birth of LLUK, further reports emerged recommending improvement to teacher education and the raising of standards within PCE (Lucas, 2004, p 35).

Equipping Our Teachers for the Future (DfES, 2004, p 5) argued that the quality of teaching affected the achievements and life chances of about '*six million learners annually in PCE*'. Later the Raising Skills, Improving Life Chances (DfES, 2006) report confirmed that the (then) Labour government was intent on reforming what it saw as a failing service. Raising the quality of teaching was also crucial to PCE providers as the funding that they received from the LSC (replaced by the SFA in 2010) was dependent upon learner achievement (Foster, 2005, p 5).

Following these reports and consultations with various stakeholders, LLUK developed a new set of standards to replace the 2001 FENTO standards. Aligned to these standards, and located in a three-tier qualification structure (levels 3, 4, 5) was a '*120 credit framework*' which contained '*core units of assessment*' (Lingfield, 2012, p 11). Previous approaches to teacher education, had, due to the political ideologies and social and economic cultures surrounding them, leaned more heavily towards teachers being qualified within their own vocational area of expertise rather than developing an understanding of '*pedagogy*' (Orr and Simmons, 2010, p 78). A report by the Skills Commission (2009) contended that education within PCE could only be as good as those teaching within it and that a qualified workforce would improve the retention and achievement of learners and enable them to work and to compete in a globalised economy and working environment.

Although LLUK recommended that teachers employed prior to 2001 become qualified, they stipulated that teachers employed after 2001 had to become qualified by 2012 and that those employed after 2007 had to become qualified within five years of starting employment. Following these changes, research (Maxwell, 2010; Noel, 2009; Orr, 2009) indicated that students were enrolling onto HEI teacher education awards from much broader backgrounds (public, private and voluntary sectors) and had a much wider range of subject backgrounds than those of the trainees prior to the changes. A teacher education model that caters for a diverse range of students was, as noted by Noel (2009, p 3), problematic as *'one size will not comfortably fit all'*; this view was also taken by Lingfield (2012).

Critical question

➤ As a teacher educator how can you offer students opportunities to develop pedagogical and subject practice?

The Institute for Learning

The Institute for Learning (IfL) was established in 2002 as a professional body for teachers working in PCE. One of its roles was to provide teachers with professionalised status through the accreditation of Qualified Teacher Learning and Skills (QTLS). Until 2007, when it was a regulatory requirement to become qualified, membership to the IfL was voluntary and funded by the government. However, the intention was for the IfL to be self-funding through dues from its members so that it could promote its integrity of being a practitioner-led body, rather than being government- or employer-led. When this happened, there was a decline in members, and the IfL eventually closed in 2014.

The Learning and Skills Improvement Service

Like FENTO, LLUK, along with SVUK and CETTs, was short-lived, and their role in relation to Teaching Standards was taken over in 2011 by the Learning and Skills Improvement Service (LSIS). LSIS, which already had some other sector development responsibilities, now shared responsibility for teacher training with the IfL, retained the LLUK standards and initially remodelled the structure of the existing three-tier qualifications. Two years later, tasked with *'simplifying and renaming the teaching qualifications'* (LSIS, 2013, p 4), LSIS introduced a new three-tier (levels 3, 4 and 5) qualification structure. However, LSIS's lifespan echoed that of its predecessors and following a review of the qualifications by Lingfield in 2012 it was, in 2013, replaced by the Education and Training Foundation (ETF).

Lingfield

A pivotal report by Lingfield (2012, p 12) announced that the *'2007 Regulations were no longer fit-for-purpose'* and that amendments to them would not *'deal adequately with their shortcomings'* and that the *'needs of diverse groups of trainees were not adequately being addressed'*. Lingfield's final report in October 2012 was not without its critics and an international consultancy organisation, commissioned by the Department for Business, Innovation and Skills, countered that the regulations were largely fulfilling their original aims of developing a professional workforce that is qualified, reflective and committed to developing a career in further education (GHK Consulting, 2012, p 7). Nevertheless, Lingfield (2012) recommended the revocation of a mandatory imposition to become qualified and professional body membership in favour of giving institutions the power to decide on what, if any, training was required for staff. According to LSIS (2013, p 4), the new approach '*did not need to rely upon government regulation but rather gave PCE some autonomy to decide the best way to raise, and to maintain, standards*'.

Critical question

➢ What teacher training or CPD have you undertaken in order to ensure that you continue to deliver high quality teacher training and CPD?

The Education and Training Foundation

The Education and Training Foundation (ETF) came about following Lingfield's recommendations for an FE Guild that would '*enhance the status of the sector by providing a single body to set professional standards and codes of behaviour*' (Lingfield, 2015, p 1). Although it replaced LSIS in August 2013, the ETF does not have ownership of the units which make up the current suite of teacher training qualifications (PCE). These have been transferred to various awarding organisations and HEIs which embed them into their own suite of qualifications.

After 2014, and the cessation of the IfL, the ETF became a single body that was '*owned by the FE and training sector*'; although notably funded by a government grant (ETF, 2015, p 1).

Society for Education and Training (SET)

In May 2015 the ETF launched a wholly owned subsidiary, namely the Society for Education and Training (SET). The aim of the SET is to '*take on the legacy of the IfL*' and to increase professional development among practitioners and the reflection of this through QTLS status (ETF, 2015, p 2).

Critical questions

➢ What approaches is the SET adopting in order to provide CPD to its members and to be able to evaluate the success of these approaches regarding teacher effectiveness?

➢ What are some of the differences between the ETF, the SET and their predecessors, ie LLUK, LSIS and IfL?

IN A **NUTSHELL**

Bursts of energy and financial input by incumbent governments into teacher education within PCE are due to their instrumentalist belief that PCE is pivotal to economic and social prosperity and is a sector that can equip a growing number of learners with the appropriate skills to compete in a global economy. Teacher educators play a key role in doing this.

REFLECTIONS ON **CRITICAL ISSUES**

Developing an understanding of the history and development of PCE and ITE can help you to make informed contributions to the community of practice to which you belong; teacher educators have a voice that can influence political and organisational change and, once made, how these changes are enacted and disseminated.

REFERENCES

Armitage, A, Bryant, R, Dunnill, R, Flannagan, K, Hayes, D, Hudson, A and Kent, J (2003) *Working in Post-Compulsory Education*. Buckingham: Open University Press.

Butler Act (1944) *The Cabinet Papers 1915–1982*. London: HMSO.

DfEE (Department for Education and Employment) (1998) *The Learning Age: A Renaissance for a New Britain*. London: DfEE.

DfES (Department for Education and Skills) (1999) *Learning to Succeed: A New Framework for Post-16 Learning*. London: HMSO.

DfES (Department for Education and Skills) (2004) *Equipping Our Teachers for the Future*. London: DfES.

DfES (Department for Education and Skills) (2006) *Further Education: Raising Skills, Improving Life Chances*. London: DfES.

DIUS (Department for Innovation, Universities and Skills) (2007) *The Further Education Teachers' Qualifications (England) Regulations 2007*. London: DIUS.

ETF (Education and Training Foundation) (2015) *About us* [online] Available at: www.et-foundation.co.uk/ (accessed September 2016).

Foster, A (2005) *Realising the Potential: A Review of the Future Role of Further Education Colleges. Report Summary*. Nottingham: DFES.

GHK Consulting (2012) *Evaluation of FE Teachers' Qualifications (England) Regulations 2007*. London: Department of Business, Innovation and Skills.

Institute for Learning (2006) *Towards a New Professionalism*, IfL Annual Conference. London: Institute for Learning.

James Report (1972) *Teacher Education and Training*. London: HMSO.

LSIS (Learning and Skills Improvement Service) (2013) *Teaching and Training Qualifications for the Further Education and Skills Sector in England: Guidance for Employees and Practitioners*. Coventry: LSIS.

Lester, S (2014) Professional versus Occupational Models of Work Competence. *Research in Post-Compulsory Education*, 19: 276–86.

Lingfield, R (2012) *Professionalism in Further Education: Interim Report*. London: Department for Business, Innovation and Skills.

Lucas, N (2004) The 'FENTO Fandango': National Standards, Compulsory Teaching Qualifications, and the Growing Regulation of FE College Teachers. *Journal of Further and Higher Education*, 28: 35–51.

Maxwell, B (2010) Teacher Knowledge and Initial Teacher Education in the English Learning and Skills Sector. *Teaching Education*, 21: 335–48.

McNair Report (1944) *Report of the Committee Appointed by the President of the Board of Education to Consider the Supply, Recruitment and Training of Teachers and Youth Leaders*. London: HMSO.

Nasta, T (2009) *The Knowledge That You Do Every Day – Easing the Transition of Those Who Enter Teaching from Vocational Backgrounds*. London: London Centre for Excellence in Teacher Training.

Noel, P (2009) *Differentiation, Context and Teacher Education: The Changing Profile of Trainees on In-service Initial Teacher Training Programmes in the Lifelong Learning Sector. A Journal to Inform and Improve Practice*. Huddersfield: University of Huddersfield Repository, pp 17–21.

Ofsted (2003) *The Initial Training of Further Education Teachers*. London: Ofsted.

Orr, K (2009) Performativity and Professional Development: The Gap between Policy and Practice in the English Further Education Sector. *Research in Post-Compulsory Education*, 14: 479–89.

Orr, K and Simmons, R (2010) Dual Identities: The In-service Teacher Trainee Experience in the English Further Education Sector. *Journal of Vocational Education and Training*, 62: 75–88.

Randle, K and Brady, N (1997) Managerialism and Professionalism in the 'Cinderella service'. *Journal of Vocational Education and Training*, 49: 121–39.

Robson, J (1998) A Profession in Crisis. *Journal of Vocational Education*, 50: 596–97.

Simmons, R and Thompson, R (2007) Aiming Higher: How Will Universities Respond to Changes in Initial Teacher Training for the Post-compulsory Sector in England? *Journal of Further and Higher Education*, 31: 171–82.

Skills Commission (2009) *Skills Commission into Teacher Training in Vocational Education*. London: Skills Commission.

Smithers, A and Robinson, P (2000) *Further Education Re-formed*. Microsoft Reader: Microsoft.

Tight, M (2002) *Key Concepts in Adult Education and Training*. London: Routledge.

Vicky Duckworth

CRITICAL **ISSUES**

- *What are the key values, approaches and principles of practice which potentially unite teacher educators (TEds) wherever they work?*

- *What are the starting points for enacting them within the professional practice of teacher education?*

Introduction

The ways in which TEds construct their professional identity is an understudied area; however, there has been significant research on teacher identity with a focus on the impact of the ways in which their work is managed and regulated (Avis, 2005; Duckworth, 2013). The research highlights the global spread of performative *'techno bureaucratic managerialism'* (Apple, 2000; Ball, 2004) and its frameworks evidenced in the studies of teachers' lives and work (Hall and Noyes, 2009; Troman et al, 2007) and post compulsory education (PCE) TEds (Duckworth et al, 2016). This chapter aims to unsettle the performative landscape that clouds many TEds' professional landscapes; in doing so it offers an alternative more socially just vision of PCE teacher education, underpinned by key uniting principles of practice, pedagogy, values and approaches which have the potential to empower and be empowering.

TEds' values, approaches and principles of practice

A range of research about TEds strongly indicates they tend to share the following values, principles and practices across all forms of teacher education and across most different locations in which it takes place (Clow and Harkin, 2009; Crawley, 2015; Harkin et al, 2008; Korthagen et al, 2005; Koster and Dengerink, 2008; Lawy and Tedder, 2012; Lucas and Nasta, 2010; Noel, 2009; Thurston, 2010).

» There is a moral role in teacher education relating to the development of inclusivity, reflexivity and social justice. TEds have a role to play in defining the visions of those areas. This often involves a strong emotional commitment to the role and its responsibilities.

» TEds model practice, ideas and situations to help teachers reflect on and develop their own perspectives and conceptualisations of teaching and professional identity.

» TEds consider supporting their students and building their confidence as central to their role.

» Developing learning communities of reflective practitioners with their students, and connecting theory, practice and the workplace through these communities also has great importance.

Teacher education and social justice

Importantly, for TEds to engage in promoting social justice this requires critical engagement which uncovers and addresses systems of power and privilege that give rise to social inequality. This engagement encourages educators to critically examine oppression on institutional, cultural and individual levels in search of opportunities for all, regardless of the communities they are born into. Ball (2004), Bowles and Gintis (1976), Hatcher (1998), Reay (2005) and Duckworth (2013) all argue that problems arising from unequal access to society's resources can be addressed through education, and in particular teacher education.

Practitioner research as a tool for the empowerment of TEds

Practitioner research (PR) has the capacity to build a meaningful approach to TEds' professional (and indeed personal) development; it has the potential to shift teachers from passive receivers of knowledge to the generators of knowledge.

There are several definitions for PR. It may be called different names, ranging from participatory action research to action research, to practitioner-led inquiry, but there are some shared characteristics that distinguish it from other research methods. PR challenges positivistic approaches to knowledge which suppose that those with distanced and 'objective' views of practice (for example, researchers from the academy) can best understand and steer practitioners (including TEds) who are seen as too close to practice to embrace an accurate perception of it (Harding, 1991). I would argue that this moves to a hegemonic understanding of knowledge where TEds cannot take ownership of and understand their own practice, but should rather seek 'experts' to make it clear it to them. This is very much a position where the institution takes control and the TEd is positioned as passive and disempowered – not a maker of knowledge. PR challenges this position and has the potential to empower and be empowering for PC TEds.

PR can be conducted by the TEd or a group of TEds, to explore uniting themes. This idea is not new and examples feature in Chapters 1 and 8 (Crawley), 2 (Dennis et al), 6 (Robinson and Skrbic) and 7 (Eliahoo). In PR I have carried out, issues related to addressing violence and trauma in the public and private lives of adult literacy learners arose from their accounts (Duckworth, 2013). These real narratives of overcoming significant barriers are now embedded into the teacher education programme in which I work, offering students examples of approaches to addressing issues of violence which permeate through many learners' lives. Stories, poetry and images were used as foils to represent the generative themes in the lives of the learners.

Importantly, what can become evident through PR is that educational research can have a ripple effect that touches and empowers the TEd, students, learners and the community. It offers a reflective and systematic approach to research and outreach that places a study setting (for example, a higher education institution (HEI), FE college or community venue) and participants (for example, TEds, students, teachers and learners) at the centre of the study. It combines the collective knowledge of the educational community, and increases the likelihood that results will be drawn upon and applied, for example, in teacher education programmes.

For many TEds, research is not a luxury that they can solely focus on; it needs to be balanced with what is often a busy teaching load and other responsibilities. PR is fundamental to developing a greater understanding of the work of PCE TEds and what happens in the classroom, but it should also enable professionals to widen their thinking and approaches to teaching and learning as educationalists. Being involved in PR allows us to come to our own understandings about our own teaching and learning. It is based on the belief that the teacher is the best judge of her or his practice in this era of compliance and delivery.

How TEds enact their values

Clearly, those who are TEds have the power to transmit their values, their world visions, their ideologies and prejudices; this makes the teaching-learning process a non-neutral one. For example, we can see our values enacted in the classroom with students. Positive relationships between students and TEds can promote a community of belongingness and care (Duckworth et al, 2016). High levels of belongingness have the potential to lead to an increase in motivation and academic achievement. Students can struggle in their journey to become confident and qualified teachers, finding the academic and practical workload overwhelming, especially if they are in-service and working full time. If they know their TEds genuinely care, believe in them and are interested in their successes it can be the difference between them completing their journey to become qualified teachers or moving away from the path. As has already been indicated in this chapter, supporting and building the confidence and autonomy of their students is central to the values, practice and pedagogy of PCE TEds (Crawley, 2015; Harkin et al, 2008; Koster and Dengerink, 2008). This is a reason why as TEds we must not shy from discussing emotions with students; we must learn about the emotions and about the emotional work involved in education because this is pivotal to teaching and learning itself. By denying this a place in our classrooms we are denying the educational needs of TEds and students (and their learners) as emotional subjects.

Supporting students to become critical practitioners

As analysed in Chapter 6 (Robinson and Skrbic) of this book, the use of modelling is an approach that works well for TEds in helping students to develop into professional teachers.

This nurturing of our students would also benefit from embracing critical pedagogical approaches where the classroom is not just about passing on knowledge, but one which embraces and promotes critical education. Many of the key components of critical and emancipatory education, including, for example, multicultural education (eg culturally responsive teaching, and cultural values and beliefs of different ethnic groups), may be viewed as abstractions to students because they have no practical experiences with them. Yet to develop socially just classrooms they need to understand the knowledge, concepts and principles in personal ways to implement them in their own classroom teaching. TEds who demonstrate critical and multicultural education principles in their own pedagogical behaviours are much more effective than those who simply talk about them. This is also true of the potential of workplace mentors, who in supporting the development of students' subject-specific pedagogy can also act as role models in their enactment of socially just practice. Duckworth and Maxwell (2015, p 17), in their exploration of how FE mentors can act as change agents for social justice, argue that this is not simplistic. Mentors may require *'training which includes raising their critical consciousnesses and developing their ability to model "good and just" teaching and act as change agents'*.

A move towards being a critical TEd is to consider our shared teaching and learning approaches with our students and whether it is within the bounds of Freirean (1993) critical pedagogy. The basis of the educational method proposed by Freire is dialogue. We can ground dialogue in our students' lives and those of their students so they can start to question dominant values that are prevalent in many discourses and practices of education. For example, oral and written linguistic capabilities are not equally valued in compulsory and post compulsory education, and even within the oral tradition, the codes of the upper classes are prioritised over the codes of working-class or ethnic minority students (Bernstein, 1971; Duckworth, 2013; Labov, 1972). This unsurprisingly means that learners who are not proficient in the linguistic skills required in FE (what Bernstein (1971) has termed the elaborated codes) are defined as failures or lacking in intelligence simply by virtue of the way they relate to and know the world (Ade-Ojo and Duckworth, 2016). By engaging in questioning and a valuing of alternative viewpoints with our students, and not on the transmission of (units of) knowledge itself, we may open up possibilities for a questioning of the taken-for-granted and normalising procedures and boundaries in which actions are enclosed.

On a fundamental level teaching, especially teacher education, is about encouraging ourselves and our students to look into our/themselves for the strength to construct new ways of seeing the world; to find the strength needed to change. It is vital to support students to recognise that for some of their learners (and indeed for our/themselves) the learning process can involve fear and shame (Duckworth, 2013). As such we need to recognise their barriers, empathise with them and meet them where they are (Ade-Ojo and Duckworth, 2016). Indeed, the only way to reach people who are fearful, lack confidence and carry shame is to show patience, establish trust, and show that we believe in them. In my experience, when I have been able to do those three things, far more students take the leap and grow personally than if I tried to force ideas on them.

Communities of practice

Communities of practice (CoPs) can be 'real' and 'virtual' and offer possibilities of critical dialogic spaces both within and out of teaching institutions for sharing and generating meaningful knowledge. The concept of communities of practice draws on a wide body of theory related to learning and sociology. It relates to a constructivist approach to learning that recognises the key importance of exchanges with others, and the role of social interactions in the construction of values and identity. Enacting teacher education values may be supported by a strong community of practice (Lave and Wenger, 1991; Wenger, 1998). As TEds we can create and join communities of practice (as exemplified in Chapters 1, 2, 6, 7 and 8 of this book in addition to this chapter) and encourage our students to do the same in their studies and in their workplaces. For example, the sharing of values in the Research and Practice in Adult Literacy (RaPAL) community includes sharing more critical approaches to teaching basic skills and thereby encourages people to reclaim their own learning processes by building their own learning from their own experiences. CoPs can offer critical space to reflect and develop on professional practice. Lave and Wenger argue that a community of practice implies *'participation in an activity system about which participants share understandings concerning what they are doing and what this means in their lives and for their communities'* (Lave and Wenger, 1991, p 98).

CoPs can build a culture of collaborative learning and sharing knowledge, which includes developing relationships between students, teachers and other participants. Members may negotiate a shared purpose through evolving interactions with one another. They might, for instance, look at teaching strategies to motivate learners and come up with a shared understanding of how they will describe what they will do together. It can also provide a safe virtual space where TEds can share their stories of their professional journeys and form empowering relationships based on shared dialogue and values. It also offers a space whereby TEds can generate professional development, which is community bound and links and connects practitioners in the same way that TEds seek to connect their students.

Reshaping teacher education as a tool for social justice

The dominant philosophy, policy and practice in FE is driven by what has been viewed as a very fertile ground for performativity (Simmons and Thompson, 2008, p 201). Ball (1990) highlights how this reductionist landscape has led to the struggle for the soul of the teacher. It is against this oppressive landscape that it is important as TEds we ask: what different value positions and, therefore, different approaches to education policy and practice are there, and what kind of society do we live in?

Bourdieu and Passeron's (1977) theories offer us explanations of educational disadvantage and, therefore, of much inequity in educational outcomes and progress of more disadvantaged students. They argue that many of the problems of society are embedded into its structures and systems, and education in particular. This can be contrasted with approaches that place greater emphasis on individual responsibility and agency (neoliberal models), and thus tend towards individualising the problem, and locate it within individual students as part of a wider discourse of deficit and failure (Duckworth, 2013). To counter this, teacher education programmes could consider embedding learning for all students about the role of cultural capital and habitus (Bourdieu and Passeron, 1997). This theoretical underpinning to practice provides a unique position for TEds, who straddle the two worlds of FE and higher education (HE), and support teachers in learning how they could become, for example, a source of social capital for learners in colleges without access to information and understanding about HE. Other elements for dialogic engagement include: valuing learners' histories and biographies within the learning environment; taking risks and confronting deficit views among peers and colleagues in the education environment. Being generators of knowledge and practice through PR enables TEds and teachers to be advocates for social justice rather than recipients of a pre-determined education programme.

Teacher education has the capacity to develop personal and professional critical consciousness and a more comprehensive understanding of the context in which education takes place. Supporting students to enhance their critical consciousness should be a major component of all forms of teacher education. As a TEd, I would argue that we have a responsibility to provide students with the skills and breadth of knowledge which they will need to be able to support learners and to instil in them the benefits of PCE.

IN A **NUTSHELL**

Transforming PCE teacher education into a socially just model requires a holistic and integrated approach. This includes care and solidarity for each other and our communities both within and external to our workplaces. Caring for each other is a fundamental prerequisite for mental and emotional well-being and indeed our development in the private and professional aspects of our lives. Recognising and standing up for our values, including working towards social justice, supporting students and finding ways of improving teaching and learning are also essential.

REFLECTIONS ON **CRITICAL ISSUES**

The greatest resource and strength in PCE is our teachers and their capacity to care. The concepts of care and caring in practice, pedagogy, values and approaches is essential in establishing rapport with our peers and students, having respect for each other and being open and accepting to other's points of view. We must not forget that a key component of this is trust; we must reclaim notions of trust and care back from performative management discourses. Enacting our values through CoPs and PR can combine to provide powerful benefits for TEds, the teachers they work with, their students and society in general. Integration of socially just values and approaches that bind and bond us is essential for this. Together we can make a difference.

REFERENCES

Ade-Ojo, G O and Duckworth, V (2016) Journey through Transformation: A Case Study of Two Literacy Learners. *Journal of Transformational Education*, 14: 1–20.

Apple, M W (2000) *Official Knowledge* (2nd edn). New York: Routledge.

Avis, J (2005) Beyond Performativity: Reflections on Activist Professionalism and the Labour Process in Further Education. *Journal of Education Policy*, 20: 209–22.

Ball, S J (1990) *Politics and Policy Making in Education: Explorations in Policy Sociology.* New York: Routledge.

Ball, S J (2004) *Class Strategies and the Education Market: The Middle Classes and Social Advantage*. London: Routledge.

Bernstein, B (1971) *Class, Codes and Control: Theoretical Studies towards a Sociology of Language, Vol. I*. London: Routledge and Kegan Paul.

Bourdieu, P and Passeron, J (1977) *Reproduction in Education, Society and Culture*. London: Sage.

Bowles, S and Gintis, H (1976) *Schooling in Capitalist America: Educational Reform and the Contradictions of Economic Life*. London: Routledge and Kegan Paul.

Clow, R and Harkin, J (2009) *The Professional Knowledge and Skills Required by New Teacher Educators in the Learning and Skills Sector*. London: Westminster Partnership CETT.

Crawley, J (2015) Growing Connections – the Connected Professional. *Research in Post-Compulsory Education*, 20: 476–98.

Duckworth, V (2013) *Learning Trajectories, Violence and Empowerment amongst Adult Basic Skills Learners*. London: Routledge.

Duckworth, V and Maxwell, B (2015) Extending the Mentor Role in Initial Teacher Education: Embracing Social Justice. *International Journal of Mentoring and Coaching in Education*, 4: 4–20.

Duckworth, V, Lord, J, Dunne, L, Atkins, L and Watmore, S (2016) Creating Feminised Critical Spaces and Co-caring Communities of Practice outside Patriarchal Managerial Landscapes. *Gender and Education*, January 2016: 1–15.

Freire, P (1993) *Pedagogy of the Oppressed*. New York: Continuum.

Hall, C and Noyes, A (2009) New Regimes of Truth: The Impact of Performative School Self-evaluation Systems on Teachers' Professional Identities. *Teaching and Teacher Education*, 25: 850–56.

Harding, S (1991) *Whose Science? Whose Knowledge? Thinking from Women's Lives*. Ithaca: Cornell University Press.

Harkin, J, Cuff, A and Rees, S (2008) *Research into the Developmental Needs of Teacher Educators for Effective Implementation of the New Qualifications for Teachers, Tutors and Trainers in the Lifelong Learning Sector in England – Draft Interim Report*. Coventry: LLUK.

Hatcher, R (1998) Class Differentiation in Education: Rational Choices? *British Journal of Sociology of Education*, 19: 5–24.

Korthagen, F, Loughran, J and Russell, T (2006) Developing Fundamental Principles for Teacher Education Programmes and Practices. *Teaching and Teacher Education*, 22: 1020–41.

Koster, B and Dengerink, J J (2008) Professional Standards for Teacher Educators: How to Deal with Complexity, Ownership and Function. Experiences from the Netherlands. *European Journal of Teacher Education*, 31: 135–49.

Labov, W (1972) *Language in the Inner City: Studies in the Black English Vernacular*. Philadelphia: University of Pennsylvania Press.

Lucas, N and Nasta, T (2010) State Regulation and the Professionalisation of Further Education Teachers: A Comparison with Schools and HE. *Journal of Vocational Education & Training*, 62: 441–54.

Lave, J and Wenger, E (1991) *Situated Learning: Legitimate Peripheral Participation*. New York: Cambridge University Press.

Lawy, R and Tedder, M (2012) Beyond Compliance: Teacher Education Practice in a Performative Framework. *Research Papers in Education*, 27: 303–18.

Noel, P (2009) *Development and Utilisation of CPD Systems and Resources for Teacher Educators*. Huddersfield: HUDCETT.

Reay, D (2005) Beyond Consciousness? The Psychic Landscape of Class? *Sociology*, 395: 911–28.

Simmons, R and Thompson, R (2008) Creativity and Performativity: The Case of Further Education. *British Educational Research Journal*, 34: 601–18.

Thurston, D (2010) The Invisible Educators: Exploring the Development of Teacher Educators in the Further Education System. *Teaching in Lifelong Learning*, 2: 47–55.

Troman, G, Jeffrey, B and Raggi, A (2007) Creativity and Performativity Policies in Primary School Cultures. *Journal of Education Policy*, 22: 549–72.

Wenger, E (1998) *Communities of Practice: Learning, Meaning, and Identity*. Cambridge, UK: Cambridge University Press.

CHAPTER 6 | INVISIBILITY OR CONNECTING PROFESSIONALS?

Denise Robinson and Nena Skrbic

CRITICAL **ISSUES**

- *Why do teacher educators (TEds) in the post compulsory education (PCE) sector seem to be invisible? or have such a low profile?*

- *How do TEds support the development of their trainees using modelling?*

- *How do TEds establish and develop their connecting role, given the barriers they face?*

Introduction

Few TEds in the PCE sector according to Gleeson et al (2005) *'can trace the roots of their profession to an established desire to teach'* (p 449). College managers also consider them to be *'the same as any other lecturer'* (Orr and Simmons, 2011, p 11). How can they then implement what they would regard as an essential element of their role – that of not only preparing new teachers but also connecting professionals in the sector? Despite being regarded by their students as skilled and dedicated, and playing a crucial role in supporting both initial teacher education (ITE) and staff development, TEds have a low visibility in teacher education overall and research on TEds is rare (see for example, Swennen and van der Klink, 2009 and Chapter 2 in this book, by Dennis et al).

While TEds are said to be 'second-order' teachers, that is, teachers of teaching (Boyd et al, 2011), those in PCE often have an additional role – that of subject specialist teacher. Research by Crawley (2013) reveals that approximately half of the TEds who responded to his survey worked on courses other than teacher education, presenting them with challenging timetables. Although extensive teaching experience in the sector is considered valuable in terms of support for subject expertise and currency, the low awareness of teacher education qualifications for the sector reinforces the seeming invisibility of the TEds themselves, whether based in further education (FE) colleges or universities. As discussed in Chapters 1, 2, 3, 5 and 8, PCE has a low public profile when compared to schools or universities, which has resulted in a *'benign neglect'* (Lucas, 2004, p 35). Policy initiatives and regulation, based on a lack of understanding and familiarity with the work of PCE, have often been perceived as ill-advised and out of touch with the realities faced by the sector.

In contrast to their counterparts in school teacher education or those in universities, PCE TEds experience further complications in that they are often teaching their colleagues and they may also be expected to conform to their own institutional learning and teaching policies (Boyd et al, 2011). These may not only place more pressure on their role as TEds but may challenge their values as teachers. So, for example, should the TEd accept the values that lie embedded in the performativity of teacher observation systems, appearing to be compliant before management, while trying to develop a profession true to its own values?

The following section explores one pedagogical construct used by TEds, that of modelling, and how this underlines effective development for students, TEds themselves and how this might raise their professional profile through enhanced engagement with the essence of teaching and learning. This is investigated through a case study of work undertaken at one FE college.

Modelling and TEds

There is increasing agreement on the purpose of the teacher education curriculum and, more particularly, intellectual support for the concept of modelling. Modelling in teacher education is highlighted as an example of outstanding practice by Ofsted. Referencing the work of one institution, a recent report records that *'the tutors on the programme demonstrate outstanding role-modelling through their practice which empowers our future teachers to be the best they can be'* (Ofsted, 2015, pp 4–5). Andrew Carter's Review (2015) forefronts the importance of the technique in the preparation of entrants to the profession, and argues that trainees should be encouraged to question the pedagogical decision-making that guides the work of the experienced teacher.

Yet modelling presents a serious challenge to the TEd and (although most theoretical accounts agree that it is a vital part of the TEd's role) a background of general scepticism is one of the factors that distinguishes the literature on this *'deceptively difficult'* (Conklin, 2008, p 661) pedagogy. The critical study of the TEd has been dominated by the notion of explicit modelling whereby TEds are expected to *'model the use of engaging and innovative teaching procedures for our students rather than "deliver" information about such practice through the traditional (and often expected) transmissive approach'* (Berry and Loughran, 2005, p 194). This is a reminder of Swennen et al's oft-quoted motto: *'teach what you preach'* (2008, p 531).

The process of modelling is however not conveniently linear; rather, there is something quite arbitrary about the way in which it is enacted by TEds and translated into praxis by trainees. To a large extent, TEds are preaching extempore. This idea of consciousness, or – more specifically – intentionality, is a recurring concept in most general discussions on modelling. For Lunenberg et al (2007): *'Little is known about the question of whether teacher educators nevertheless succeed in serving as role models for their students, and whether they do so consciously'* (p 589). This comment offers up a number of salient questions regarding the degree to which TEds are aware of the factors that underpin their pedagogical choices.

Case study

An analysis was undertaken of a new, re-designed course of teacher preparation at one urban FE college, which captures the many-sidedness of the debate around teacher educator modelling. The re-design of the pre-service and in-service teacher education curricula necessitated a fundamental change in the way teacher education is practised and experienced at the college. It involved investigating, re-thinking and re-evaluating the emphasis that was placed on modelling. From the beginning a key decision was made to write modelling into the educational aims of the programme. This was an initial attempt to ensure that the department shared a commitment to its enactment in more than a casual and oblique way.

The curriculum review was built on the four-stage typology of teacher development provided by McDonald et al (2013). The stages are as follows:

(a) Stage 1. Representation: watching others teach;

(b) Stage 2. Approximation: planning for teaching;

(c) Stage 3. Enactment: teaching in practice; and

(d) Stage 4. Investigation: reflecting on practice (ibid, p 382).

TEds reflected this typology – first and foremost, by giving trainees the opportunity to observe the teaching of others; then, to enable the trainee to plan and develop their own pedagogical content knowledge with a view to the third stage of enactment. Finally, critical reflection was necessary for an understanding of practice. Our aim was no less than to re-form the curriculum to give precedence to the first stage of the typology.

The re-design of the curriculum raised a number of important questions regarding identity and the construct of self-efficacy. We expect TEds to model, but the ability to do so depends on various conditions – not least the personal theories that TEds hold about their practice. Indeed, the question of self often re-emerges in discussions of the TEd's role. For Berry and Loughran (2005), modelling '*demands considerable awareness of oneself, pedagogy and students*' (p 193). In a similar vein, White writes about the psychological journey of becoming a TEd (White, 2014). Self-knowledge is an essential preliminary to successful modelling and this idea of consciousness is connected to Berry and Loughran's notion of '*see[ing] into practice*' (2005, p 200), which will be explored in the next section.

Mirrors, metaphors and invisibility

In 'Modelling by Teacher Educators' (2005), Loughran and Berry set up a crucial motif of mirror-imaging: '*This is at the heart of what modelling really means. Laying bare one's own pedagogical thoughts and actions for critique and doing so to help student–teachers "see into practice" – all practice, not just the good things we do*' (p 200). The metaphor of '*seeing into practice*' established by Loughran and Berry is a revelatory one. Here, the authors establish a much more metaphoric definition of the TEd's role. On the one hand, their function is to establish that vital mimetic (or representational) contact between theory and practice. On the other hand, the mirror motif raises questions about artificiality and constructedness. Indeed, modelling has particular implications in the rhetoric of the catwalk and theatre, fashioning the work of the TEd as an overtly artful rather than artless performance. Since modelling relates to acting a part, to individual style and self-exposure, this level of auto-awareness can engender a feeling of vulnerability, which was an important factor to consider in the review process.

Teaching about pedagogy is a complex (and often unreliable) craft. As Hagger et al (2008) argue:

What happens to beginning teachers when the support structures and resources of their teacher education programmes are no longer there and they are obliged to function as real teachers? Are they equipped to go on learning in new and diverse contexts?

(Hagger et al, 2008, p 174)

Invisibility, a metaphor that relates directly to the title of this chapter, suggests a mirror that has lost its power of reflection and for the TEd – as the foregoing citation suggests – there is no such thing as a precise mirroring, since his or her frame of reference can never be the totality of a trainee's experience. The analogy of the mirror must, ultimately, break down, reflecting a context that is only partially knowable to the TEd. So, why model at all? There are other less challenging (and potentially more reliable) forms of mimesis (eg video analysis, practical criticism of case studies) after all.

Such troublesome questions aside, the re-design did contribute to a genuine advance in our understanding of the process. Four particularly significant insights emerged from it.

1. The propositional knowledge needed by practising TEds is not clearly established.

2. A consensus on the key areas of practice to model must be achieved.

3. Formal training, including development of the capabilities and dispositions of a researcher, would enhance TEds' capacity to implement modelling in their classrooms.

4. Opportunities for modelling must be properly organised and conducted on lines appropriate to the initiative and particular interests of the teacher education team.

The interchange of ideas on methods and techniques during the re-design process helped to promote a better understanding of each other's work and indeed the technical complexity of teacher education pedagogy. Being a TEd requires a cross-range of skills and the longer-term opportunities for collaboration are substantial. It is anticipated that further development of the curriculum will exploit the interesting possibilities that are available for a cross-disciplinary approach to teacher education or '*cross-professional pedagogy*' (Dotger, 2010, p 805). Another emerging factor at the curriculum development stage was the professional learning of the TEd, more specifically, the considerable know-how requisite in developing teacher-educator-mediated practices. Modelling may be a '*desirable professional competency*' (Loughran and Berry, 2005, p 193), but what support is available to engender this vital skill? To this end, the review highlighted the importance of continuous and progressive training in a range of teacher-educator-mediated strategies (in particular, in-the-moment coaching, co-teaching and co-generative dialoguing) and sensitivity to the contextual dimension of the TEds' work. Modelling cannot be viewed in isolation from the institutional realities of our under-provisioned sector.

Until the principles for effective modelling are written into the teacher education curriculum, we will not have a consistent approach to its application or any degree of intentionality guiding the degree to which modelling is planned. The TEd (and this is a general charge that can be applied to TEds from all sectors) belongs to a rather free-form, undifferentiated category and there is a sense in which this lack of definition can be seen to perpetuate rather than surmount the barriers to explicit modelling of practice.

Critical questions

- ➢ How aware are TEds of the factors that underpin their pedagogical choices?
- ➢ How can TEds support the enactment of theory in practice (Russell, 2007)?
- ➢ How is unconscious modelling (White, 2011) of, for example, professional relationships with colleagues and assumed values recognised and explained?

TEds: Connecting professionals

From this discussion around modelling and its application to the development of a specific PCE programme, questions about formal recognition, preparation for the role and CPD emerge. While this chapter cannot offer a full exposition, it provides a consideration of how TEds maintain their position as 'connecting professionals'. Two possibilities are offered:

1. one which focusses on values, thereby challenging the outcomes and evidence-based approach;
2. one which is based on Aristotle's 'phronesis' or practical wisdom.

There is an argument that these should become embedded in future TEd standards, if developed (see Chapter 5, Duckworth and Chapter 7, Eliahoo).

Values versus evidence-based practice

Despite the variation in approaches to theory, curriculum and pedagogy (which may be considered a strength rather than a weakness), one aspect of teacher education which can be regarded as maintaining and acting as a role model is that of values. This is crucial in the face of the exhortation for all teaching to be evidence based. This is the challenge of developing new teachers on the basis of evidence which, it is claimed, results in better teachers. Biesta (2007) has made a powerful argument that challenges this thinking. This is a discourse based on our understanding of knowledge; Biesta refers to Dewey's (1859–1952) transactional theory of knowing whereby learning is acquired through responding to problems that require thinking and action – we cannot know the answer to a problem until we have both thought and acted upon our thoughts, '*we can only ever acquire knowledge as a result of our actions*' (Biesta, 2007, p 15). For professional action to be successful we must recognise that the problem is unique and, while past experience can provide a basis from which we can explore a resolution to the new problem, it will not provide an exact answer. Evidence will only provide '*hypotheses for intelligent problem solving*' (Biesta, 2007, p 17).

The way forward is to think, explore, act and, through the '*pedagogy of wandering*' (Gale, 2003, p 174), maintain an openness of mind that can result in a creative development. This provides a fundamental challenge to the tips and formulaic practices sometimes envisioned in policy stances (for example, Gove, 2010). The danger of evidence-based practice is that it can become a route to received wisdom, a recycling of '*uncontroversial statements of what should be known*' (Simmons and Thompson, 2007, p 177) and a method of reproducing '*bureaucratic virtues such as compliance and the collection of evidence*' (Ellis, 2010, p 106). The TEd needs to break free from these as opposed to embracing them. In summary, Biesta (2012, p 45) underlines the role of values in teacher education:

the formation of the teacher should be oriented towards a certain 'virtuosity' with regard to making concrete situated judgements about what is educationally desirable.

Phronesis

Our next offering is based on Aristotle's (Aristotle, [Ross and Urmson, 1980]) phronesis or practical wisdom and is an extension of a values-based approach. This kind of wisdom or knowledge is differentiated from that of episteme (absolute knowledge) or techne (instrumental knowledge). For Eisner (2002, p 375) the aim of phronesis '*is to arrive at good but imperfect decisions with respect to particular circumstances*'. This underlines teaching as a unique interaction between teacher and student with experience as a counter-play rather than a strict adherence to specific strategies. We are familiar with the benefits of reflection and Schön's (1987) reflection-in-action which emphasises the crucial role of reflection as a way to improve practice and there is a very good reason why this has become so well established in teacher education courses. Phronesis clearly relates theory, experience and practice. It highlights the tentative, temporary and contextualised nature of our work and that the search for the one formulaic answer is a chimera. This may present problems for the TEd faced with students seeking certainty and comfort in the face of the daunting task of entering the teaching profession. However, phronesis is '*practical reasoning based on judgements and wisdom*' (Plowright and Barr, 2012, p 2). Phronesis can become a powerful tool to use on a teacher education programme.

Critical questions

➣ How might a values-based approach to teacher education conflict with evidence-based approaches? What has been your experience?

➣ Should modelling be written into general ITE practices and objectives?

➣ Is there scope for a cross-disciplinary approach to ITE?

IN A **NUTSHELL**

This chapter has highlighted the vagaries of the TEd's position as a seemingly invisible yet crucial role in the FE and Skills sector. Modelling has been examined and work cited from ongoing research. Two approaches in the development of TEds have been presented which, in particular, underline values-based teaching.

REFLECTIONS ON **CRITICAL ISSUES**

The issues raised in this chapter are ones that emerge on occasions when TEds have the 'luxury' of extending their discourse beyond the typical concerns over professional standards, grading, observation feedback and the like. Yet the issues surrounding modelling, pedagogy, values-based versus evidence-based practice and phronesis (practical wisdom) are surely core to the essence of teacher education. In the buffeting of policy change, should TEds not have a deeper understanding and debate about such matters in order to withstand and defend their role as the educators of the profession?

Until the principles for effective modelling are written into the teacher education curriculum we will not have a consistent approach to its application. The TEd (and this is a general charge that can be applied to TEds from all sectors) belongs to a rather free-form, ill-defined category and there is a sense in which this lack of definition can be seen to perpetuate rather than surmount the barriers to explicit modelling of practice. This chapter has also raised questions to do with the serviceableness of the teacher education curriculum and has forefronted the need for innovation on a rather more fundamental level.

REFERENCES

Aristotle [Ross, W D, and Urmson, J O] (1980) *The Nicomachean Ethics*. Oxford: Oxford University Press.

Biesta, G (2007) Why 'What Works' Won't Work: Evidence-based Practice and the Democratic Deficit in Educational Research. *Educational Theory*, 57: 1–22.

Biesta, G (2012) Giving Teaching Back to Education: Responding to the Disappearance of the Teacher. *Phenomenology & Practice*, 6: 35–49.

Boyd, P, Harris, K and Murray, J (2011) *Becoming a Teacher Educator: Guidelines for Induction* (2nd edn). Bristol: Escalate, HEA.

Carter, A (2015) *Review of Initial Teacher Training*. London: Department of Education.

Conklin, H G (2008) Modelling Compassion in Critical, Justice-Oriented Teacher Education. *Harvard Educational Review*, 78: 652–706.

Crawley, J (2013) Endless Patience and a Strong Belief in What Makes a Good Teacher: Teacher Educators in Post-compulsory Education in England and Their Professional Situation. *Research in Post-Compulsory Education*, 18: 336–47.

Dotger, B (2010) 'I Had No Idea': Developing Dispositional Awareness and Sensitivity through a Cross-professional Pedagogy. *Teaching and Teacher Education*, 26: 805–12.

Eisner, E W (2002) From Episteme to Phronesis to Artistry in the Study and Improvement of Teaching. *Teaching and Teacher Education*, 18: 375–85.

Ellis, V (2010) Impoverishing Experience: The Problem of Teacher Education in England. *Journal of Education for Teaching*, 36: 105–20.

Gale, K (2003) Creative Pedagogies of Resistance in Post Compulsory (Teacher) Education, in Satterthwaite, J, Atkinson, E and Gale, K (eds) *Discourse, Power, Resistance*. Stoke on Trent: Trentham Books, pp 165–74.

Gleeson, D, Davies, J and Wheeler, E (2005) On the Making and Taking of Professionalism in the Further Education Workplace. *British Journal of Sociology of Education*, 26: 445–60.

Gove, M (2010) *Speech to the National College Annual Conference*, 16 June, Birmingham, UK.

Hagger, H, Burn, K, Mutton, T and Brindley, S (2008) Practice Makes Perfect? Learning to Learn as a Teacher. *Oxford Review of Education*, 3: 159–78.

Loughran, J and Berry, A (2005) Modelling by Teacher Educators. *Teaching and Teacher Education*, 21: 193–203.

Lucas, N (2004) The FENTO Fandango: National Standards, Compulsory Teaching Qualifications and the Growing Regulation of FE College Teachers. *Journal of Further and Higher Education*, 28: 35–51.

Lunenberg, M, Korthagen, F and Swennen, A (2007) The Teacher Educator as a Role Model. *Teaching and Teacher Education*, 23: 586–601.

McDonald, M, Kazemi, E and Kavanagh, S (2013) Core Practices and Pedagogies of Teacher Education: A Call for a Common Language and Collective Activity. *Journal of Teacher Education*, 64: 378–86.

Ofsted (2015) *Good Practice Example: Initial Teacher Education (ITE) – Edge Hill University*. London: Ofsted.

Orr, K and Simmons, R (2011) Restrictive Practice: The Work-Based Learning Experience of Students in English Further Education Colleges. *Journal of Workplace Learning*, 23: 243–57.

Plowright, D and Barr, G (2012) An Integrated Professionalism in Further Education: A Time for Phronesis? *Journal of Further and Higher Education*, 36: 1–16.

Russell, T (2007) How Experience Changed My Values as a Teacher Educator, in Russell, T and Loughran, J (eds) *Enacting a Pedagogy of Teacher Education: Values, Relationships and Practices*. Abingdon: Routledge, pp 182–91.

Schön, D A (1987) *Educating the Reflective Practitioner*. San Francisco, CA: Jossey-Bass Publications.

Simmons, R and Thompson, R (2007) Aiming Higher: How Will Universities Respond to Changes in Initial Teacher Training for the Post-compulsory Sector in England? *Journal of Further and Higher Education*, 31: 171–82.

Swennen, A and Van der Klink, M (eds) (2009) *Becoming a Teacher Educator: Theory and Practice for Teacher Educators*. Amsterdam: Springer Science and Business Media.

Swennen, A, Lunenberg, M and Korthagen, F (2008) Preach What You Teach! Teacher Educators and Congruent Teaching. *Teachers and Teaching*, 14: 531–42.

White, E (2011) Working towards Explicit Modelling: Experiences of a New Teacher Educator. *Professional Development in Education*, 37: 483–97.

White, E (2014) Being a Teacher and a Teacher Educator – Developing a New Identity? *Professional Development in Education*, 40: 436–49.

CRITICAL **ISSUES**

- *Which dispositions do teacher educators (TEds) share around the world?*
- *How and why have other countries developed support, standards or guidance for TEds?*
- *What can we learn from this?*

Introduction

After a decade as a lecturer in a further education (FE) college, I was asked to team teach on an introductory teacher education course. Officially putting my toe in the TEd pool, I experienced teacher education from the other side and began to share the values and approaches of this community.

The first rule seemed to be: don't let anything faze you, whether you are observing teaching practice in hospital operating theatres, factories and army assault courses or on a farm handling small animals. You have to be flexible in terms of timetabling, willingness to explore new areas – and clothing. A colleague said that her Navy trainee asked her to observe him teaching underwater. She duly donned a dry suit and recorded the observation at the bottom of a pool, using an adapted pencil.

Despite working in a professional context which is to some degree unique, TEds in PCE share many recognisable characteristics, experiences, values and approaches – and indeed skills and knowledge – with other TEds around the world. Other countries have, however, developed ways of embedding these into more structured standards or support for TEds.

As part of a PhD, I studied the professional development needs of TEds in English PCE (Eliahoo, 2014) and explored the ways in which they were recruited, inducted and supported, in order to gain insights into how these aspects of practice could be strengthened or improved in the future. This chapter considers global perspectives on teacher education in schools, colleges and higher education (HE) and draws together examples of professional development and support for TEds which post compulsory TEds can learn from.

The dispositions of TEds

In 2012, a group of seven TEds in the USA posed a question to themselves: '*if I turn a mirror on myself, am I going to do the same things that I'm chastising teachers for doing in my classroom?*' (Pennington et al, 2012, p 69).

Drawing on Katz and Raths (1985) who introduced the term '*disposition*' in the mid-1980s, Pennington et al highlighted firstly, the importance of positive professional dispositions in teaching and secondly, the lack of knowledge about the dispositions of TEds themselves (Zeichner, 2007). Their analysis was intended as a call to examine teacher educator dispositions and to reflect more profoundly on TEds' own attitudes and identities (Pennington et al, 2012, p 81).

A further desirable disposition of TEds is the necessity for self-awareness and critical evaluation of one's practice. This is argued in research by TEds in Australia, the USA and Europe (Bair et al, 2010; Berry, 2008; Pennington et al, 2012; Swennen et al, 2008), and by Dennis et al in Chapter 2 and Duckworth in Chapter 5.

Murray and Male (2005) studied the challenges that new school TEds face establishing their professional identities in English HE. They described TEds as '*second order*' teachers (Murray and Male, 2005) because they teach about teaching and because they model practice for their students to make links between theory and practice explicit.

TEds in English PCE

Research about PCE TEds has also contributed to identifying their dispositions and approaches. Crawley (2014) and Eliahoo (2014) both found that TEds had a good understanding of their own professional values and motivation and used this to work with their trainees. TEds argue that they need to remember why they came into the profession and why they are prepared to deal with its pressures.

Crawley (2014) and Eliahoo (2014) also find examples where TEds sustain a democratic management style, not only with their students, but with their course team, in order to maintain positive power relations within the team and to sustain their own agency and credibility.

A further disposition is the development of augmented skills in interpersonal relationships, diplomacy, tact and the ability to resolve conflict, in order to be able to communicate with their students as adult to adult. TEds need to be able to motivate their trainees but still retain their respect (Crawley, 2014; Eliahoo, 2014).

Harkin et al (2008) found that PCE TEds are generally chosen from a pool of teachers who are already considered to be good or outstanding in their current field. Theirs is a '*triple professionalism*' as subject expert, teacher and TEd with a passion for teaching and learning. Chapters 1 (Crawley) and 2 (Dennis et al) argue they need an '*even more*' quality because it is their role to represent and synthesise an overview of teacher education; act as role models who innovate and share good practice; support colleagues' professional development; and critically engage and collaborate with a wide range of teachers and learners.

This fusion of collaborative role, modelling good practice and creation of a support network makes the professional role complex and multidimensional. In order to be successful, TEds must be able to make the transition from pedagogy to andragogy, since they have to work with staff and colleagues, as well as providing accurate, challenging and helpful feedback on teaching practice (Crawley, 2014; Eliahoo, 2014).

Helping PCE TEds understand and develop these dispositions has not been given priority in the organisation and support of English PCE teacher education. Research into more clearly defining TEds and their dispositions, and actions to support the development of these dispositions has however taken place in other countries.

Global examples of work to support and develop TEds

Professional standards in the USA

In 1992, the US Association of Teacher Education (ATE, 1992) started a process to identify, regularly revise and apply standards for TEds, which is still in place today. Ducharme and Ducharme (1996) identified four reasons for serious, sustained study of TEds:

1. Teacher education's presence and place in US HE in the 1990s and the role and status of TEds were somewhat problematic and contentious.

2. Teacher education has substantive ties to schools as sites of ITE research.

3. Critics of ITE in the USA based their negative images on blanket condemnation and hearsay rather than scholarly inquiry and study of TEds.

4. There was a lack of knowledge about those who educate teachers and what they do.

The Netherlands

The Dutch Association of Teacher Educators (DATE) started their own project 'The Professional Quality of Teacher Educators' in 2007. This required participants to self-assess against the Dutch standards for TEds (DATE, 2011) and undertake appropriate professional development, after which they were registered as certified TEds by DATE (Koster and Dengerink, 2008; Koster et al, 2008). Those involved saw the Dutch Standard as having two functions (Koster and Dengerink, 2001, p 346):

1. an internal function providing TEds with professional development and enhanced practice;

2. an external function which reassured stakeholders – such as students, employers and parents – that TEds would reach a certain level of professional competency and quality.

But DATE questioned whether individual TEds could embody all the different competencies.

The Dutch Standard focussed on knowledge and skills *'because attitudes, personal characteristics or motives are not very tangible'* (Koster et al, 2005, p 159).

Koster and Dengerink (2001) recommended that it should be TEds themselves who should screen and update their standards and professional competences at least every two years – otherwise, they said, TEds would *'lose their right to ownership'* (2001, p 354) and standards would be imposed on them. Further research highlighted the need to study the relationship between the competence of TEds and an increase in the quality of teachers (Koster et al, 2008). By developing, clarifying and implementing professional standards themselves, Dutch TEds made an important contribution to their own continuous professional development and to raising the policy debate about European standards for TEds (Koster and Dengerink, 2001; Snoek et al, 2011).

Israel

In Israel, Kari Smith proposed three reasons to support the professional development of TEds:

To improve the profession, teacher education;

To maintain interest in the profession, to grow personally and professionally;

To advance within the profession, promotion.

(Smith, 2003, p 203)

Smith also identified practical suggestions for the development of TEds through:

higher academic degrees;

in-service workshops and seminars outside the teacher education institution;

staff development inside the teacher education institution;

feedback on teaching;

voluntary and forced support;

peer tutoring.

(Smith, 2003, p 205)

She saw the professional development of TEds as *'an unavoidable process'* (Smith, 2003, p 213), and concluded that there are distinct differences between skilled teachers and skilled TEds (2005). She stressed their importance to the educational system as a whole, since TEds act as models for new teachers and as practitioners in the continuous process of lifelong learning. They should therefore attend international seminars and conferences to present and receive feedback on their research, as well as investing in professional relationships beyond their own institutional and national borders.

Why have English TEds failed to produce their own standards?

In England, at the time of publication, PCE TEds have not developed professional standards. American academic Linda Darling-Hammond (2010) asserted that school teacher education was at a major crossroads between two models: a professionalism approach and accelerated certification programmes, such as Teach for America (similar to Teach First in England). She saw the situation for TEds as the best of times and the worst of times:

It may be the best of times because so much hard work has been done by many teacher educators over the past two decades to develop more successful program models ... It may be the worst of times because there are so many forces in the environment that conspire to undermine these efforts.

(Darling-Hammond, 2010, p 35)

In 2006, the former United Kingdom education sector skills council, Lifelong Learning UK (LLUK), proposed a set of standards for TEds. They were narrowly focussed and vague statements, presenting LLUK's instrumental view of the essential qualities, characteristics and knowledge of TEds (LLUK, 2007). They failed to gain support, particularly from the TEds themselves, and sank without a trace.

A combination of factors has disheartened TEds in PCE:

>» a forced diet of ever-changing government policy over three decades;

>» a procession of different Ministers, Secretaries of State and civil servants in government departments with responsibility for education, skills and training;

>» the ebb and flow of regulatory instructions from government departments or regulatory bodies which becomes captured in an ever-changing set of acronyms: FENTO, LLUK, QIA, LSIS and ETF (respectively, Further Education National Training Organisation, Lifelong Learning UK, Quality Improvement Agency, Learning and Skills Improvement Service, the Education and Training Foundation);

>» a follow-the-money approach by FE colleges whose Byzantine funding mechanisms leave them vulnerable to the vagaries of the market;

>» successive governments' decisions to bequeath standards and competences from above, rather than negotiating an evolving and holistic approach with TEds themselves.

The metamorphosis from teacher to TEd

The transition from teacher to TEd is not straightforward, but complex and messy. TEds' dilemmas are not necessarily resolved, but managed; and moving between identities is a significant learning experience.

A rocky road in Australia

Denise Wood and Tracey Borg examined the transition that classroom teachers experience when they start to metamorphose into TEds in Australia. They undertook a form of self-study to analyse themselves and their experiences in the hope of proposing new strategies for their university to support the transition of new TEds (2010, p 18).

Referring to the conflicts and tensions experienced by TEds as *'the rocky road'*, they explored the challenges of transition. These included grappling with changed levels of autonomy, institutional isolation, new technologies, the pressure to enter the research culture and the impact of individual internal pressures (Wood and Borg, 2010). Beginning TEds' views could oscillate from euphoria to pessimism – perhaps because of the demands of their own context and institution; or perhaps because of aspects of their own personality, including their coping mechanisms and personal resilience.

Wood and Borg felt that it was vital for organisations and individual TEds to recognise this oscillating rocky road towards a new professional identity and to put in place strategies and processes to address this, such as mentoring; professional development in teacher education; and support for research.

Only connect: How to avoid a 'seat of the pants' approach to scholarship

Research evidence suggests that TEds struggle to overcome simplistic perceptions of teaching and learning as the transmission of information, tips and tricks, rather than the generation of research and scholarship around teacher education pedagogy (Loughran, 2011; Lunenberg et al, 2011).

The comparatively low status of teacher education within PCE may lead beginning TEds to accept high teaching loads at the expense of space and time for pedagogical research. Yet the scholarship of teaching is vital for the credibility of TEds who must develop their trainees' powers of reasoning about their practice, otherwise a vicious cycle reinforces the status quo (Loughran, 2011, p 284).

In his examination of aspects of his transition from classroom teacher to TEd, Zeichner (2005) criticised a lack of knowledge about the literature in teacher education leading to a *'seat of the pants'* approach to running teacher education programmes. He recommended that new TEds involve themselves in self-study and critique of their practice as well as engaging in greater depth with the conceptual and empirical literature in teacher education.

Becoming TEds in Canada: an English-inspired idea

In Toronto, Clare Kosnik, Yiola Cleovoulou, Tim Fletcher, Tiffany Harris, Monica McGlynn-Steart and Clive Beck were part of a three-year initiative, *Becoming Teacher Educators* (BTE). Most new TEds in Canada were not inducted or supported in any significant way (Kosnick et al, 2011). Inspired by the work of British academic, Jean Murray, in schools teacher education, a group of 12 doctoral students, who wanted to become TEds, along with two professors, formed the BTE study group to address the logistics of teacher education (such as assignments) as well as more nebulous issues of professional identity. Their three-year initiative resulted in a strong community with shared leadership; opportunities to develop knowledge of teacher education; and opportunities to improve research skills and improve practice. This informal, but safe, setting allowed them to share thoughts and questions as well as exploring their fears, and dealing with the challenges and surprises of teacher education (Kosnik et al, 2011).

Dancing in the ditches: Australia's Quality Teaching Action Learning project

Similarly, in Australia, *Quality Teaching Action Learning* was a professional development project which encouraged collaboration between 3 academic partners and 35 school teachers in 2003, in order to improve practice (Reynolds et al, 2013). The project arose from the assumption that the quality of teaching in classrooms has a strong and direct effect on the overall quality of education for students. Individual schools were encouraged to identify areas of need and to develop projects to assist in improving the quality of teaching and learning.

The collaborative projects were designed to get everyone out of their comfort zone and 'dancing in the ditches' – an uncomfortable place that often holds unexpected dangers in Australia. The metaphor was designed to describe the spaces where the groups interacted and worked through issues together. Teachers saw the TEds' role as a practical, or technical, activity which aimed to get a specific job done in order to achieve certain goals. The TEds agreed, but saw themselves in a more mediating role which centred on being more reflexive than the teachers. What emerged from the project was that TEds have a substantial and transformative role that requires extensive expertise.

IN A **NUTSHELL**

Beginning TEds often lack support in their struggle with changing professional identity. The 'rocky road' that they might experience may be seen either as a rite of passage, or as a stumbling block. But other countries are showing the way forward through self-study, collaborations, do-it-yourself (DIY) professional standards and substantive research – pointing to a future where PCE TEds will be inducted, mentored and supported within a collaborative and expansive network of colleagues.

REFLECTIONS ON **CRITICAL ISSUES**

TEds across the world have identified dispositions and approaches to teacher education, depending on TEds' context and experience. These 'second-order' professionals possess certain dispositions and if they can be supported to map their experiences, skills and attributes to professional standards and 'professional profiles' of their own devising, PCE TEd communities might feel empowered to emulate other countries' models and take their professional development into their own hands.

REFERENCES

ATE (Association of Teacher Education) (1992) Standards for teacher educators. [online] Available at: www.ate1.org/pubs/uploads/tchredstds0308.pdf (accessed 23 June 2016).

Bair, M A, Bair, D E, Mader, C E, Hipp, S, and Hakim, I (2010) Faculty Emotions: A Self-study of Teacher Educators. *Studying Teacher Education*, 6: 95–111.

Berry, A (2008) *Tensions in Teaching about Teaching: Understanding Practice as a Teacher Educator.* Dordrecht: Springer.

Crawley (2014) *How can a deeper understanding of the professional situation of LLS teacher educators enhance their future support, professional development and working context?* PhD Thesis. Bath: Bath Spa University.

Darling-Hammond, L (2010) Teacher Education and the American Future. *Journal of Teacher Education*, 61: 35–47.

DATE (Dutch Association of Teacher Educators) (2011) Knowledge base of teacher educators. [online] Available at: www.lerarenopleider.nl/velon/about-velon/ (accessed 23 June 2016).

Ducharme, E and Ducharme, M (1996) Development of the Teacher Education Professoriate, in Murray, F B (ed) *The Teacher Educators' Handbook: Building a Knowledge Base for the Preparation of Teachers*. San Francisco: Jossey Bass.

Eliahoo, R (2014) *The accidental experts: A study of FE teacher educators, their professional development needs and ways of supporting these.* PhD Thesis. London: UCL/Institute of Education.

Harkin, J, Cuff, A and Rees, S (2008) *Research into the Developmental Needs of Teacher Educators for Effective Implementation of the New Qualifications for Teachers, Tutors and Trainers in the Lifelong Learning Sector in England – Draft Interim Report.* Coventry: LLUK.

Katz, L G, and Raths, J D (1985). Dispositions as Goals for Teacher Education. *Teaching and Teacher Education*, 1: 301–7.

Kosnik, C, Cleovoulou, Y, Fletcher, T, Harris, T, McGlynn-Stewart, M and Beck, C (2011) Becoming Teacher Educators: An Innovative Approach to Teacher Educator Preparation. *Journal of Education for Teaching: International Research and Pedagogy*, 37: 351–63.

Koster, B and Dengerink, J (2001) Towards a Professional Standard for Dutch Teacher Educators. *European Journal of Teacher Education*, 24: 343–54.

Koster, B, Brekelmans, M, Korthagen, F and Wubbels, T (2005) Quality Requirements for Teacher Educators. *Teaching and Teacher Education*, 21: 157–76.

Koster, B and Dengerink, J (2008) Professional Standards for Teacher Educators: How to Deal with Complexity, Ownership and Function. Experiences from the Netherlands. *European Journal of Teacher Education*, 31: 135–49.

Koster, B, Dengerink, J, Korthagen, F and Lunenberg, M (2008) Teacher Educators Working on Their Own Professional Development: Goals, Activities and Outcomes of a Project for the Professional Development of Teacher Educators. *Teachers and Teaching*, 14: 567–87.

LLUK (Lifelong Learning UK) (2007) *Further Education Workforce Reforms: Explaining Initial Teacher Training, Continuing Professional Development and Principals' Qualifications in England*. Coventry: Lifelong Learning UK.

Loughran, J (2011) On Becoming a Teacher Educator. *Journal of Education for Teaching: International Research and Pedagogy*, 37: 279–91.

Lunenberg, M, Korthagen, F and Zwart, R (2011) Self-Study Research and the Development of Teacher Educators' Professional Identities. *European Educational Research Journal*, 10: 407–20.

Murray, J and Male, T (2005) Becoming a Teacher Educator: Evidence from the Field. *Teaching and Teacher Education*, 21: 125–42.

Murray, J, Czerniawski, G and Barber, P (2011) Teacher Educators' Identities and Work in England at the Beginning of the Second Decade of the Twenty-first Century. *Journal of Education for Teaching*, 37: 261–77.

Patrizio, K M, Ballock, E and McNary, S W (2011) Developing as Teacher Educator-Researchers. *Studying Teacher Education: A Journal of Self-study of Teacher Education Practice*, 7(3): 263–79.

Pennington, J L, Brock, C H, Abernathy, T V, Bingham, A, Major, E M, Wiest, L R and Ndura, E (2012) Teacher Educators' Dispositions: Footnoting the Present with Stories from Our Pasts. *Studying Teacher Education: A Journal of Self-Study of Teacher Education Practices*, 8: 69–85.

Reynolds, R, Ferguson-Patrick, K and McCormack, A (2013). Dancing in the Ditches: Reflecting on the Capacity of a University/School Partnership to Clarify the Role of a Teacher Educator. *European Journal of Teacher Education*, 36: 307–19.

Smith, K (2003) So, What about the Professional Development of Teacher Educators? *European Journal of Teacher Education*, 26: 201–15.

Smith, K (2005) Teacher Educators Expertise: What Do Novice Teachers and Teacher Educators Say? *Teaching and Teacher Education*, 21: 177–92.

Snoek, M, Swennen, A and van der Klink, M (2011) The Quality of Teacher Educators in the European Policy Debate: Actions and Measures to Improve the Professionalism of Teacher Educators. *Professional Development in Education*, 37: 651–64.

Swennen, A, Lunenberg, M and Korthagen, F (2008) Preach What You Teach! Teacher Educators and Congruent Teaching. *Teachers and Teaching*, 14: 531–42.

Wood, D and Borg, T (2010) The Rocky Road: The Journey from Classroom Teacher to Teacher Educator. *Studying Teacher Education*, 6: 17–28.

Zeichner, K (2005) Becoming a Teacher Educator: A Personal Perspective. *Teaching and Teacher Education*, 21: 117–24.

Zeichner, K (2007) Accumulating Knowledge across Self-studies in Teacher Education. *Journal of Teacher Education*, 58: 36–46.

CRITICAL **ISSUES**

- *What have we learned about post compulsory teacher education and teacher educators (TEds)?*

- *'Growing connections' in post compulsory education (PCE) and beyond.*

- *Building a PCE TEd community of 'connecting professionals'.*

Introduction

This concluding chapter firstly reflects on what we have learned from this book about PCE teacher education and PCE TEds. A picture has emerged of the particular context, values, pedagogy and professional identity of a field which has been little researched. The cumulative research, reflections and assertions within the book demonstrate not only that we are still 'becoming' TEds, but that we are also moving towards becoming 'first-order' professionals with a growing confidence. The chapter then continues by advancing the notion of 'growing connections' or using small, local networks and alliances as the key to building a more visible and unified community of TEds and teachers for the future.

The book closes by considering how this progress can be built upon beyond the personal, local and national boundaries of this one group of TEds, suggesting that this is essential as we enter an 'even more' turbulent and challenging future than the period we have just experienced.

PCE TEds: embedded and entangled

Every chapter of this book has referenced the complex and challenging terrain which is PCE, and how the strongly managerial and constantly changing environment, combined with a *'discourse of derision'* (Ball, 1990) inevitably also proves problematic for teacher education and TEds. The future holds the prospect of more challenging times, even though the past eight years has already been a highly austerity-focussed period of cuts and further change. A 2015 Select Committee report into the *'financial sustainability'* of further education (FE) colleges found that *'the declining financial health of many colleges is potentially damaging for learners and local economies'* (House of Commons, 2015, p 5). The committee also raised serious concerns about the newly established 'area reviews' of colleges, and whether *'they are fair, and that they result in consensus on sustainable solutions to meet local needs'* (HoC, 2015, p 6).

This same Select Committee also voiced support for what Orr (Chapter 3) describes as the *'tremendous transformative power of PCE'* (p 31) when indicating that *'4 million learners per year'* benefit from FE colleges, and that they are an *'important local presence'* (HoC, 2015, p 6). As has often been the case in recent times, on the one hand government is undermining teacher education, while on the other hand appearing to support its purpose. This contradictory and confusing approach from government results in what Machin, Chapter 4, characterises as *'bursts of energy and financial input'* (p 32) rather than any sustained, strategic approach.

As many PCE TEds are employed in and by colleges or other PCE providers, and also tend to teach their original subject specialism they had before they moved into teacher education (Crawley, 2013), they could be described as 'embedded' in their work context. Being in this situation inevitably means however that they are also 'entangled' in the context of the sector within which they work.

Murray (2008, p 18) asserts that TEds remain an *'under-researched and poorly understood occupational group'*. In Chapter 2 (Dennis et al), Chapter 5 (Duckworth) and Chapter 6 (Robinson and Skrbic), the respective authors reinforce that perspective and argue that there is a subgroup of TEds which receives 'even less' research attention, and that is PCE TEds. It is reasonable therefore to ask who defines this professional group? Is it the sector itself? Is it the organisational context? Is it the visibility of its members in research? Is it power and influence? Is it the teacher trainees with whom we work? Is it ourselves as practitioners and people?

The truth, as this book and other research (Al-Saaideh and Tareef, 2011; Arremen and Weiner, 2007; EC, 2010; Misra, 2011; Skills Commission, 2010; UNESCO, 2008) suggests, is that it can be all of these or none of these. As a result of the research undertaken by the authors of this book and others, it has however been possible, even within this embedded and entangled professional situation, to locate evidence of what the roles, dispositions, values and approaches of PCE TEds are. This book has drawn together some of the evidence and arguments involved.

Supporting, modelling, championing, becoming and connecting

Supporting and connecting other teachers

Frank Coffield (2008) asked the question *'just suppose teaching and learning became the first priority?'* For PCE TEds, and indeed for many other TEds, it is. There is a consensus on the high degree to which PCE TEds are focussed on the needs of their trainees in PCE-based research (Clow and Harkin, 2009; Crawley, 2013; Lawy and Tedder, 2009; Noel, 2006; Sampson, 2009), and international research on other TEds agrees (Danaher et al, 2000; Davey, 2013; Menter et al, 2010; Murray, 2004).

Dennis et al (Chapter 2), Duckworth (Chapter 5) and Robinson and Skrbic (Chapter 6) all accept that PCE TEds are embedded in their work situation, but argue this can be used as a positive catalyst to promote a greater reflexivity in TEds and students, and stronger connections between them as a group of professionals. As a learning process this can help students reframe their experiences and shift their perspectives and practices towards a new, more autonomous and open approach to their teaching. As Dennis et al suggest this embeddedness *acknowledges experience, context and a commitment to being excellent to the nth degree* (p 14).

Modelling

Modelling is a recognised and important aspect of teacher education, and in Chapter 6, Robinson and Skrbic contend that modelling *demands considerable awareness of oneself, pedagogy and students* (Loughran and Berry, 2005, p 193). They emphasise that modelling can be *revelatory* both for trainees and TEds, and that it can focus both on the *practical wisdom* suggested by Aristotle's 'phronesis' and values, and supporting students to stand up to some of the pressures and contradictions they face in their daily work in PCE. In Chapter 2, Dennis et al agree that modelling is central to teacher education and that it can both explicitly demonstrate different aspects of practical teaching, and promote reflection on broader themes such as what education is for and why this could be argued to be the case. Robinson and Skrbic (Chapter 6) and Eliahoo (Chapter 7) discuss how modelling could be a recognised component of a set of defining characteristics of, or professional standards for TEds if developed.

Championing democratic social justice

Teacher education research has strongly emphasised the civic responsibilities of TEds to broader objectives of social justice and democratic responsibility (Bentley, 2009; Cochran-Smith, 2004; Iredale et al, 2013; Koster and Dengerink, 2008). Zeichner (2009) also emphasises a responsibility to act for change and to put social responsibility and justice into action.

Duckworth (Chapter 5) considers how supportive and open relationships formed with trainees can create collaborative, democratic spaces for critical reflection. By encouraging teachers to act as social justice advocates, this can foster a passion for social justice; and support students in developing inclusive critical pedagogies. This argument runs strongly throughout this book, and as Zeichner argues, *'the goal of greater social justice is a fundamental part of the work of teacher education in democratic societies, and we should never compromise on the opportunity to make progress on its realisation'* (2009, p 160).

Agility, flexibility and constant 'becoming'

The 'rocky road' of PCE is explored by Eliahoo in Chapter 7, and is argued by Orr in Chapter 3 as fostering a real impetus for PCE TEds to adopt an agile and flexible approach where *'to cope and thrive, teacher education and teacher educators (TEds) need to manage constant change while maintaining a commitment in their practice to their own professional values*' (p 21). Some aspects of the work of teacher education, such as learning theory, curriculum content and how many trainees are recruited are more under the control of TEds themselves than in primary and secondary teacher education (Clow and Harkin, 2009; Crawley, 2014; Tummons, 2014). This does give them aspects of autonomy not enjoyed by all TEds. This partial autonomy, developed agility and flexibility, in combination with previous (and ongoing) accumulated experience of being a teacher can all be deployed as a powerful force within teacher education. As Dennis et al (Chapter 2) argue, these factors combine to leave TEds in an almost permanent state of transition or 'becoming'. They are '*between being a teacher educator and actually feeling like a teacher educator*' (p 11). This is one of the factors which led to Murray and Male (2005) using the term '*second order teachers*' with respect to TEds. Perhaps PCE TEds can never be expected to arrive at the point of 'being' a teacher educator. Perhaps they may never be described as 'first-order' teachers. Within the '*swampy lowlands*' (Schön, 1983, p 42) that constitute PCE, a position of ongoing reflection, development and 'becoming' can however be seen as an advantage rather than a disadvantage. The way in which their own embedded and entangled position is used by TEds to help teachers make connections and expand their own practice is the key to why Robinson and Skrbic (Chapter 6) and Crawley (2015) call them '*connecting professionals*'.

Overall, the difficult to define but expansive role, characteristics and disposition of PCE TEds is one where they constantly need to be '*even more*' than (Crawley, 2013) or '*more than*' (Swennen, 2014) the teachers they train. They also need to be '*connecting professionals*'. This '*evenmoreness*' and their mission to connect other teachers are perhaps their defining characteristics.

Growing connections

We have now arrived at a good understanding of PCE TEds, and we would hope it has become apparent that the authors of this book represent a visible and coherent voice which deserves to be heard and recognised. As has been discussed in most chapters, achieving this goal in a sector such as PCE is far from straightforward, so how can this evenmoreness and capacity to connect be further enacted, nurtured and grown?

'*Growing connections*' is a term devised by Crawley (2015) which is based on an approach to the design of technology-supported CPD constructed by Laurillard and Ljubojevic (2011). It has at its essence the concept of using reflection on critical incidents, which most of us are familiar with from writers such as Hillier (2012) and Schön (1983). In this particular case the key emphasis is on devising small ideas, activities and incidents through collaboration and then sharing those further among their own community of practice. If teachers are to adopt an innovation, whether using technology, or in any other field, they need to feel it will be useful and they need to have some indication why that will be the case. If these small changes and innovations are shared and understood by all, and all seek to apply the resulting learning, the results are more likely to become embedded in the practice of one or more of the participants.

In Chapter 5, Duckworth also suggests approaches which can contribute to growing connections, and provides examples, and they are contained within the concept of Practitioner Research (PR). In Chapter 7, Eliahoo provides a range of examples of how we have learned from small projects, activities and innovations across the world, and how it could now be an opportune time to undertake similar projects in PCE, and to use these to help set standards for TEds which we would have constructed ourselves from our own work to grow connections. As Robinson and Skrbic (Chapter 6) suggest, '*the way forward is to think, explore, act*' through '*the pedagogy of wandering*' (Gale, 2003, p 174) in order to maintain an '*openness of mind that can result in a creative development*' (p 47).

Growing connections in action

Sharing Innovation in Teacher Education (SITE) project

In 2011–12, a small project managed by a team of PCE practitioner researchers successfully tested out the '*growing connections*' approach. A panel of 'expert teacher educators' constructed a catalogue of innovatory teacher education activities which they had utilised in their own programmes, and which had been evaluated as successful by TEds and trainees (and in one or two cases Ofsted – through an inspection which was taking place while the project was running). This innovation catalogue was then made available to teacher education teams from two universities, two FE colleges, one private training provider, and one regional infrastructure support organisation, all in the south-west of England. The teams selected two items from the catalogue, used them in their own provision, evaluated them internally then shared those evaluations at a facilitated discussion meeting at SWCETT. The project engaged with some 16 TEds and in excess of 150 teacher trainees during the eight months of operation. The results strongly supported the growing connections approach and included findings that:

» a significant majority of the innovations were felt to have worked well;

» the activities added value to and improved the quality of teacher education programmes;

» participants would use the activities again;

» the supportive facilitation of project networking and evaluation helped participants actively engage.

The project's final report argued that the way the project operated was '*an approach which could in general work well in many other aspects of the professional life of teachers in the (PCE) sector*' (Crawley, 2012, p 11).

Going global

In Chapter 7, Eliahoo's guided tour of examples of and ideas about teacher education professional development across the world provides us with some powerful food for thought, and suggests some prospective further connections which could be made in the name of PCE teacher education. Connecting with other TEds may just be the way to help us continue to develop as this book suggests we have been. It may well now be time, as Eliahoo recommends, for PCE TEds to '*feel empowered to emulate other countries' models and take their professional development into their own hands*' (p 57).

IN A **NUTSHELL**

Even more 'evenmoreness'

I would like to thank the contributors to this book for bringing this series of positive perspectives about a neglected field to the reader in a way which we hope you have found encouraging and possibly inspiring.

We do not wish to underestimate the task which lies ahead, as the future of the whole PCE sector is under threat at the time of writing. We will survive the future only if we act to ensure that we continue to develop as critically reflexive professionals so we can help our trainees to do the same. This will involve being even more committed to our work with teachers; even more of a community of practice; even more together as a group and even more confident in asserting our own identity and values to others.

In short, in extremely trying times, PCE teacher education, and PCE TEds, need even more 'evenmoreness'.

REFLECTIONS ON **CRITICAL ISSUES**

The team of authors behind this book, and the other colleagues in the TELL research network have contributed in ways which represent PCE TEds as committed, expansive and value-driven professionals. They are engaging more with research and development, and continuing to improve the outcomes of their trainees (ETF, 2015).

PCE teacher education has become more resilient and we have better and perhaps slightly more valued teacher education and a more confident and outward-looking community of TEds. In such a non-nurturing environment this represents good progress.

REFERENCES

Al-Saaideh, M and Tareef, A (2011) Vocational Teacher Education Research: Issues to Address and Obstacles to Face. *Education*, 131: 715–31.

Arreman, I E and Weiner, G (2007) Gender, Research and Change in Teacher Education: A Swedish Dimension. *Gender and Education*, 19: 317–33.

Ball, S J (1990) *Politics and Policy Making in Education: Explorations in Policy Sociology*. New York: Routledge.

Bentley, D (2009) Daring to Teach Teachers: Passion, Politics and Philosophy in Post-compulsory Teacher Education, in Appleby, Y and Banks, C (eds) *Looking Back and Moving Forward: Reflecting on Our Practice as Teacher Educators*. Preston: UCLan, pp 79–86.

Clow, R and Harkin, J (2009) *The Professional Knowledge and Skills Required by New Teacher Educators in the Learning and Skills Sector*. London: Westminster Partnership CETT.

Cochran-Smith, M (2004) Defining the Outcomes of Teacher Education: What's Social Justice Got to Do with It? *Asia-Pacific Journal of Teacher Education*, 3: 193–212.

Coffield, F (2008) *Just Suppose Teaching and Learning Became the First Priority* … London: Learning and Skills Network.

Crawley, J (2012) *South West Centre for Excellence in Teacher Training (SWCETT) – Sharing Innovation in Teacher Education (SITE) Project Report*. Taunton: South West Centre for Excellence in Teacher Training.

Crawley, J (2013) Endless Patience and a Strong Belief in What Makes a Good Teacher: Teacher Educators in Post-compulsory Education in England and Their Professional Situation. *Research in Post-Compulsory Education*, 18: 336–47.

Crawley, J (2014) *How can a deeper understanding of the professional situation of LLS teacher educators enhance their future support, professional development and working context?* PhD Thesis. Bath: Bath Spa University.

Crawley, J (2015) Growing Connections – the Connected Professional. *Research in Post-Compulsory Education*, 20: 476–98.

Danaher, P A, Gale, T and Erben, T (2000) The Teacher Educator as (Re)Negotiated Professional: Critical Incidents in Steering between State and Market in Australia. *Journal of Education for Teaching*, 26: 55–71.

Davey, R (2013) *The Professional Identity of Teacher Educators: A Career on the Cusp?* London: Routledge.

EC (European Commission) (2010) *The Profession of Teacher Educator in Europe*. Report of a Peer Learning Activity in Reykjavik, Iceland, 21–24 June 2010. Brussels: EC.

ETF (Education and Training Foundation) (2015) *Initial Teacher Education Provision in FE and Skills: Baseline Report*. London: ETF.

Gale, K (2003) Creative Pedagogies of Resistance in Post Compulsory (Teacher) Education, in Satterthwaite, J, Atkinson, E and Gale, K (eds) *Discourse, Power, Resistance*. Stoke on Trent: Trentham Books.

Hillier, Y (2012) *Reflective Teaching in Further and Adult Education* (3rd edn). London: Continuum.

HoC (House of Commons) (2015) *Overseeing Financial Sustainability in the Further Education Sector – Public Accounts Committee*. London: House of Commons.

Iredale, A, Bailey, W, Orr, K and Wormald, J (2013) Confidence, Risk, and the Journey into Praxis: Work-based Learning and Teacher Development. *Journal of Education for Teaching: International Research and Pedagogy*, 39: 197–208.

Koster, B and Dengerink, J J (2008) Professional Standards for Teacher Educators: How to Deal with Complexity, Ownership and Function. Experiences from the Netherlands. *European Journal of Teacher Education*, 31: 135–49.

Laurillard D and Ljubojevic D (2011) Evaluating Learning Designs through the Formal Representation of Pedagogical Patterns, in Kohls, J W and Kohls, C (eds) *Investigations of E-Learning Patterns: Context Factors, Problems and Solutions*. Hershey, PA: IGI Global, pp 86–105.

Lawy, R and Tedder, M (2012) Beyond Compliance: Teacher Education Practice in a Performative Framework. *Research Papers in Education*, 27: 303–18.

Loughran, J and Berry, A (2005) Modelling by Teacher Educators. *Teaching and Teacher Education*, 21: 193–203.

Menter, I, Hulme, M, Elliott, D and Lewin, J (2010) *Literature Review on Teacher Education in the 21st Century*. Glasgow: University of Glasgow.

Misra, P K (2011) VET Teachers in Europe: Policies, Practices and Challenges. *Journal of Vocational Education & Training*, 63: 27–45.

Murray, J (2004) *Professional Educators in the English University Sector: A Comparison of Teacher Educators' Professional Practices with Those of Medical, Social Work and Nurse Educators*. Research Study for the Universities Council for the Education of Teachers (UCET) 2004. London: UCET.

Murray, J (2008) Teacher Educators' Induction into Higher Education: Work-Based Learning in the Micro Communities of Teacher Education. *European Journal of Teacher Education*, 31: 117–33.

Murray, J and Male, T (2005) Becoming a Teacher Educator: Evidence from the Field. *Teaching and Teacher Education*, 21: 125–42.

Noel, P (2006) The Secret Life of Teacher Educators: Becoming a Teacher Educator in the Learning and Skills Sector. *Journal of Vocational Education and Training*, 58: 151–70.

Sampson, A (2009) *The Issues Facing In-service Initial Teacher Training in the Post-compulsory Sector with Specific Regard to Teachers of Vocational Subjects or Practical Skills*. London: Westminster Partnership CETT.

Schön, D (1983) *The Reflective Practitioner: How Professionals Think in Action*. New York: Basic Books.

Skills Commission (2010) *Teacher Training in Vocational Education*. London: Skills Commission.

Swennen, A (2014) More Than Just a Teacher: The Identity of Teacher Educators, in Jones, K and White, E (eds) *Developing Outstanding Practice in School-based Teacher Education*. Northwich: Critical Publishing.

Tummons, J (2014) Professional Standards in Teacher Education: Tracing Discourses of Professionalism through the Analysis of Textbooks. *Research in Post-Compulsory Education*, 19: 417–32.

UNESCO / International Reading Association (2008) *State of Teacher Education in the Asia-Pacific Region*. Newark, USA: UNESCO.

Zeichner, K M (2009) *Teacher Education and the Struggle for Social Justice*. London: Routledge.

INDEX